363.34   Allen, Missy.
ALL
           Dangerous natural
           phenomena.

                              11BT01060

$19.95

363.34   Allen, Missy.
ALL
           Dangerous natural
           phenomena.

                  11BT01060

$19.95

DATE	BORROWER'S NAME		

BAKER & TAYLOR

DANGEROUS
NATURAL PHENOMENA

The Encyclopedia of Danger

DANGEROUS ENVIRONMENTS

DANGEROUS FLORA

DANGEROUS INSECTS

DANGEROUS MAMMALS

DANGEROUS NATURAL PHENOMENA

DANGEROUS PLANTS AND MUSHROOMS

DANGEROUS PROFESSIONS

DANGEROUS REPTILIAN CREATURES

DANGEROUS SPORTS

DANGEROUS WATER CREATURES

CHELSEA HOUSE PUBLISHERS

The Encyclopedia of Danger

DANGEROUS NATURAL PHENOMENA

Missy Allen

Michel Peissel

CHELSEA HOUSE PUBLISHERS

New York   Philadelphia

The Encyclopedia of Danger includes general information on treatment and prevention of injuries and illnesses. The publisher advises the reader to seek the advice of medical professionals and not to use these volumes as a first aid manual.

On the cover   Photograph of a tornado on its path of destruction

Chelsea House Publishers

Editor-in-Chief   Richard S. Papale
Executive Managing Editor   Karyn Gullen Browne
Copy Chief   Philip Koslow
Picture Editor   Adrian G. Allen
Art Director   Nora Wertz
Manufacturing Director   Gerald Levine
Systems Manager   Lindsey Ottman

The Encyclopedia of Danger
Editor   Karyn Gullen Browne

Staff for DANGEROUS NATURAL PHENOMENA
Associate Editor   Terrance Dolan
Copy Editor   Danielle Janusz
Production Editor   Marie Claire Cebrián-Ume
Editorial Assistant   Laura Petermann
Designer   Diana Blume
Picture Researcher   Pat Burns

3   5   7   9   8   6   4

Library of Congress Cataloging–in–Publication Data

Peissel, Michel.
Dangerous natural phenomena/by Michel Peissel and Missy Allen.
p.   cm.—(The Encyclopedia of danger)
Includes bibliographical references and index.
Summary: Provides a brief description of twenty–five natural phenomena (drought, dust devil, el niño, mud slide, lightning, monsoon, etc.), possible damage each may cause, different forms of prevention, and survival instructions.
ISBN   0-7910-1794-X
       0-7910-1938-1 (pbk.)
1. Weather—Juvenile literature. 2. Weather control—Juvenile literature. 3. Natural disasters—Juvenile literature. [1. Natural disasters. 2. Weather.] I. Allen, Missy. II. Title. III. Series: Peissel, Michel, 1937– Encyclopedia of danger.

QC981.3.P45 1993
363.3'492—dc20

92–18980
CIP
AC

CONTENTS

DANGEROUS NATURAL PHENOMENA

One has only to turn on the evening news to get a full dose of dangerous phenomena; the nightly broadcasts are filled with accounts and images of war, civil unrest, fires, earthquakes, and other disasters. This volume, however, will examine only those dangerous phenomena that are visited on humankind by nature—although many of these misfortunes are inevitably compounded by the actions of humans. (A book detailing the disasters that humankind visits upon itself would no doubt take decades to complete and would probably be too heavy to carry out of a bookstore.)

The majority of dangerous natural phenomena examined here are weather related. Some of these phenomena—such as blizzards, cyclones, hurricanes, monsoons, and thunderstorms—can be viewed as extreme manifestations of weather itself. A wide variety of secondary but no less dangerous manifestations can also be attributed to weather conditions: these secondary phenomena include fog, lightning, flash floods, snow, hail, tornadoes, high winds, and even mud slides and avalanches set in motion by heavy rains or snow. Dangerous natural phenomena such as glaciers, icebergs, anomalous ocean currents, and droughts are also the products of long-term meteorological patterns and conditions.

Those dangerous natural phenomena not related to weather conditions are for the most part seismic or tectonic (of or related to movements of the earth's crust) in origin. These cataclysmic events—earthquakes, volcanoes, and tsunamis—are the result of immense forces and energies at work within the earth, and they are perhaps the most awesome and frightening of natural phenomena because they are powerful enough to reshape the very face of the planet. They can cause the earth to heave and tremble and the oceans to rear up and reclaim islands; they level forests, conjure blizzards of ash, and turn day into night.

It is conceivable that someday meteorologists and other scientists might learn how to influence the weather and thus prevent or at least lessen the destructive force of phenomena such as hurricanes, thunder-storms, and tornadoes. Research toward these goals has already been going on for decades. But it is doubtful that humans will ever learn how to prevent earthquakes, volcanoes, and tsunamis. These events are like acts of the gods; they seem as inevitable, inscrutable, and unforgiving as fate itself. Indeed, they are a fact of life on this planet. But another seemingly unquestionable fact is the resiliency of *Homo sapiens*. No matter how violent the earthquake or how great the flood, it seems that somewhere beneath the rubble, or perhaps clinging to a piece of wood adrift on the floodwaters (or traveling more comfortably aboard an ark), there are always survivors—people hoping for a new day and a chance to start rebuilding.

KEY

INJURY/ILLNESS/TRAUMA

MILD

MODERATE

SEVERE

FATAL

CLIMATE

ARCTIC TEMPERATE TROPICAL

MATERIAL DAMAGE

SLIGHT

MODERATE

SEVERE

CATASTROPHIC

KEY

PRIMARY ENVIRONMENT

INDOORS

OUTDOORS

UNDERGROUND

AQUATIC

MOUNTAINS

URBAN

VEHICLE

UBIQUITOUS

INCIDENCE

RARE

INFREQUENT

FREQUENT

VICTIMS

INDIVIDUAL

GROUP

AVALANCHE

INJURY/ILLNESS/
TRAUMA

CLIMATE

PRIMARY
ENVIRONMENT

VICTIMS

INCIDENCE

MATERIAL DAMAGE

When a forestry worker in Glarus, Switzerland, was seized by a powder avalanche and flung through the air, he thought that his flight had taken but a split second. Actually he had been carried over half a mile. "Head sometimes upward, head sometimes downward like a leaf driven by a storm," he was blasted by snow from all sides. He could not see, could scarcely breathe, and lost consciousness before he was dropped into deep snow, which broke his fall and limited his injuries to a few fractures.

Although an avalanche victim buried in wet snow usually has only about 22 minutes to live, there are exceptions. An Austrian postman was buried for three days before being rescued. He owed his life to his loyal and insistent dog, who convinced rescuers that his master was still alive.

Avalanche

During World War I an estimated 60,000 soldiers were killed by avalanches on the Alpine front, many deliberately set off by enemy artillery fire. Bodies were still being recovered in the early 1950s. An Austrian ski-troop instructor stated that the mountains were "more dangerous than the Italians."

Perhaps the greatest loss of life from a single avalanche occurred on January 10, 1962, when more than three tons of snow and ice roared down the slopes of Huascarán, one of the highest peaks in the Andes Mountains, into the inhabited Peruvian valley below. A small town was destroyed and over 4,000 people were killed. The worst avalanche in U.S. history occurred near Wellington, Washington, on March 1, 1910; it swept a snowbound train over a ledge and into a canyon 150 feet below. One hundred and eighteen passengers were killed.

Name/Description

The word *avalanche* is derived from *avalantse* (to alter), which comes from a French dialect in the northwestern Alps. An avalanche is a large mass of snow and ice in swift motion down a mountainside or over a precipice. Avalanches are frequent occurrences in the Alps, the Himalayas, the Rockies, the Caucasus, the Andes, and the Pyrenees; the biggest avalanches occur in the mostly uninhabited Himalayas. Human suffering caused by avalanches is greatest in the Alps (there are 10,000 avalanche paths in Switzerland alone), especially in the vulnerable valleys, which are often relatively densely populated.

Some avalanches are set in motion after the foundations of snow masses have been loosened by spring rains or foehns (warm, dry mountain winds). Others are caused by large cornices (overhanging masses of compacted snow) that break off when they become too heavy. Both types of avalanche can be initiated by vibrations caused by artillery fire, thunder, blasting, or even a single skier. Avalanches can hurtle along at speeds of up to 225 miles per hour.

Wet-snow avalanches are considered most dangerous because of their great weight and their tendency to quickly solidify when motion

11

stops, thus entombing any victims in an icy crust. Dry, or powder avalanches are dangerous because they carry along great quantities of air that allow the powdery snow to behave like a fluid, often flowing up the opposite side of a narrow valley like an ocean wave.

Injury/Illness/Trauma

Most avalanche victims die within a short period of time from suffocation, bodily injury, or shock. In general, there is only a 50-50 chance of survival for a victim buried in the snow for half an hour; after two hours, most victims, even those with only minor injuries, succumb to exposure and hypothermia. (See Injury/Illness/Trauma page, 104.)

Material Damage

Material damage caused by avalanches is relatively minimal because they occur mostly in unpopulated areas. However, an avalanche can bury a village in seconds. Avalanches can also interrupt or destroy communication and transport lines.

Prevention

Organizations such as the Snow and Avalanche Research Institute of Switzerland investigate methods of detecting potential avalanches. A traditional method of averting disastrous avalanches in populated areas is to relieve the snow buildup by triggering smaller avalanches with explosives. This is a risky practice, however; there has been a tendency to overdo the amount of explosives used. In some areas, forest barriers and deflection structures have been erected, but they are ineffective in large avalanches. Skiers and other people who travel in avalanche country often carry radio transmitters, which emit signals—even through thick snow—to guide rescue workers. Other sophisticated electronic devices have been developed to help locate victims buried in deep snow.

Avalanche

An avalanche victim has about 22 minutes to live when buried in wet snow.

Survival

- If you find yourself downhill from an avalanche, flatten yourself against a tree, boulder, or any other anchored object you can find.

- Tie an avalanche cord or any length of brightly colored material around you to aid rescuers in finding you.

- If you are swept away, keep your head up and out of the snow. Lie on your back or stomach and maintain a powerful swimming motion with both arms.

- If you are buried, try to create as much air space as possible around your face and chest.

BLIZZARD

INJURY/ILLNESS/
TRAUMA

CLIMATE

PRIMARY
ENVIRONMENT

VICTIMS

INCIDENCE

MATERIAL DAMAGE

In early March 1888 the northeastern United States was blessed with springlike weather; baseball fields were occupied on sunny days. For March 11, weather services predicted rains with "gentle southeasterly winds." However, a winter cyclone raced southeastward from the Great Lakes, covering 600 miles a day. Another storm developed in the Gulf of Mexico and then moved northward up the Atlantic coast. The two storms collided and stalled over New York City. The temperature fell quickly, from the high 40s to the mid–20s, and 70–mile–per–hour winds drove snowdrifts 20 feet high against the New York City brownstones. At the time, the country was in the throes of a minidepression. Employment was scarce and wages were low, so those who had jobs struggled to work that Monday morning. One New Yorker described his harrowing attempt to return home from work: "I stumbled along, falling down at almost every step, burying myself in the snow when I fell, struggling frantically up only to sink down deep again. Then I began to feel like a crazy man. Every time I fell down, I shouted and cursed and beat the snow with my fists. I was out there all alone, and I knew it." On the third day of the blizzard, temperatures plummeted into the single digits and men built fires to melt passageways through the frozen snowdrifts. Four thousand people died, 200 in New York City alone.

A more recent killer blizzard began on February 15, 1958, and clogged the Great Lakes region. Moving south with temperatures in the teens, 45-mile-per-hour winds, and gusts of up to 60 miles per hour, the storm deposited 10-foot snowdrifts in the suburbs of Baltimore and Washington, D.C. Wayne County, Pennsylvania, was buried under 42 inches of snow, and citizens of Syracuse, New York, had to dig their way out from under 61 inches. One hundred and seventy-one people died from Maine to Alabama, mostly from exertion and exposure. Near the Morgantown Interchange of the Pennsylvania Turnpike almost 800 people found themselves stranded in a restaurant. Panic set in when they learned that there was only enough food for 100. Luckily, nearby Amish farmers distributed bologna and cheese for a modest fee to adults and free to children. Although the restaurant was only 45 minutes from Philadelphia, it remained cut off from relief for 36 hours.

Name/Description

The word *blizzard* most likely comes from the German word *blitz*, meaning "lightning." In 19th-century America, *blizzard* meant a violent strike or blow such as a musket shot. In 1834 the American frontiersman Davy Crockett wrote about "taking a blizzard" at some deer. A newspaper editor in Iowa was the first person to use the word to describe a blinding snow storm.

A blizzard is a cyclonic winter storm usually occurring in temperatures below 20 degrees Fahrenheit, in which strong horizontal winds blow at 35 miles per hour or more, driving large amounts of fine, dry snow. A blizzard does not require an actual snowfall to be occurring; the blowing of snow that has already fallen is sufficient to cause high snowdrifts and extremely poor visibility.

During a blizzard, high winds cause the snow to become dry and powdery and thus less prone to stick; snow blowing across open ground may remain suspended in the air until the winds die down. But the windblown snow will pile up, sometimes into enormous drifts, against the windward surfaces of natural barriers or structures. Narrow roads between hedges can be filled to overflowing with snow—as was the case in the March 1991 blizzard in Devon, England—while the exposed fields on either side remain almost devoid of settled snow. Drifts can freeze into compacted, rippled formations, called *sastrugis*, which make traveling extremely difficult if not impossible.

Injury/Illness/Trauma

Most fatalities during blizzards are from exposure and/or exertion, although some victims have been known to suffocate under the powdery snow. (See Injury/Illness/Trauma, page 104.)

Material Damage

See Snow, page 76.

Prevention

The National Weather Service gives fairly accurate winter storm warnings. (See Disaster Preparation and Survival, page 106.)

Survival

- If you are trapped in a car during a blizzard, use whatever materials are at hand to survive. A traveling salesman buried in his car in a 1978 blizzard in Scotland survived by making the most of what he had with him. He maintained a fresh air supply by poking a stick up through the snow and kept starvation at bay with a meager supply of cookies. The

Blizzard

During a blizzard in Buffalo, New York, in February 1977,
20-foot-high drifts became so compacted that the
blades of snowplows broke on them.

salesman managed to keep from freezing to death by wrapping himself in the product he was selling—ladies' tights.

- Run the car engine and heater *sparingly*; move around as much as possible to maintain circulation and ward off frostbite and hypothermia; keep the inside light on for rescuers to see; and try to remain awake.

- Be alert for symptoms of hypothermia. (See Injury/Illness/Trauma, page 104.)

- If you are caught out in the open during a blizzard, seek shelter immediately (avoiding exertion if possible) and stay inside until the storm abates.

CYCLONE

INJURY/ILLNESS/
TRAUMA

CLIMATE

PRIMARY
ENVIRONMENT

VICTIMS

INCIDENCE

MATERIAL DAMAGE

For Abdul Hadi and countless other inhabitants of the Ganges–Brahmaputra delta region of Bangladesh, there is nowhere to hide. Hadi now lives in a bamboo and corrugated-tin hut that is much like the one that disappeared in the cyclone of May 1985 along with his wife and four of his children. When the cyclone hit, 100–mile-per-hour winds pushed a 50–foot-tall storm surge into the Bay of Bengal, flooding the coast and hundreds of islands.

An estimated 100,000 people died, 30,000 cattle were killed, and 3,000 square miles of cropland were ravaged. Huts like Hadi's, hastily erected on *chars* (little islands of mud and silt that form after the annual flooding

18

of the Ganges and Brahmaputra rivers subsides), were quickly destroyed by the wind and water, along with the chars themselves. As his hut was swept away, Hadi grabbed two logs and placed them under his armpits. Seizing two of his sons, he was carried out and away by the waters.

Miraculously, Hadi and his two sons survived. But many others did not. As Hadi, his sons, and other survivors gathered in a relief center to collect biscuits, water, and corrugated tin to build new huts, Hadi shrugged and said, in resignation, "Where else can I go? What Allah has done is done." It was the 60th killer cyclone to strike Bangladesh since 1822. These cyclones have claimed a total of 1.6 million lives.

Name/Description

In 1848, Captain H. Piddington of the Royal Navy first used the word *cyclone* (from the Greek *kyklos*, meaning "circle"), to describe intense circular storms in the Indian Ocean. Cyclones, like hurricanes and typhoons, develop from tropical depressions, low–pressure weather systems with a warm central core. Cyclonic winds spin inward toward the low–pressure center. Cyclones have a counterclockwise rotation in the Northern Hemisphere and a clockwise rotation in the Southern Hemisphere. The converging air currents move upward, expanding and cooling, forming clouds and bad weather.

Cyclones usually advance at about 20 to 30 miles per hour, have a radius of 90 to 100 miles, and bring abundant precipitation and high winds. (The maximum wind gusts ever observed during a cyclone occurred in March 1968 when Cyclone Monique struck the island of Rodriguez, 300 miles due east of Mauritius in the Indian Ocean. Gusts of up to 173 miles per hour were recorded.) Most cyclones are spawned over the Indian Ocean and then move up the Bay of Bengal.

Injury/Illness/Trauma

Most cyclone fatalities are due to drowning or massive injury caused by waterborne or airborne debris and collapsing structures. The risk of

Gusts of up to 173 miles per hour have resulted from cyclones.

illness, sometimes on an epidemic scale, is great following a cyclone because water supplies are usually contaminated. During the 1985 cyclone in Bangladesh, wells and streams were tainted over a 1,961 square-mile area. In countries such as Bangladesh, medical supplies are often inadequate or unavailable. Devastation of crops and destruction of transportation systems results in widespread famine. (See Injury/Illness/Trauma, page 104).

Prevention

The greatest problem is money. A country like Bangladesh, where much of the population lives below the poverty line, does not have the resources to implement preventive measures. Just weeks before the 1985 disaster, an international team had installed a highly sophisticated radio warning system. But most Bangladeshis could not afford radios. Bangladesh does have a law—which has proved almost impossible to enforce—that chars cannot be settled for 10 years, in order to allow the government to plant and raise trees that will anchor the land during flooding. More concrete structures are needed instead of the traditional bamboo and tin huts. Rescue helicopters are vital as well. During a recent cyclone in Bangladesh, the government had only eight helicopters for rescue and evacuation operations. Outdated military helicopters could be donated by other, more prosperous nations.

Survival

- The only escape from a cyclone is to seek high ground, although in Bangladesh most of the coastline land is at sea level and thus there is no "high ground" to speak of. In some areas, artificial hills have been built for this purpose. (See Disaster Preparation and Survival, page 106.)

DROUGHT

INJURY/ILLNESS/
TRAUMA

CLIMATE

PRIMARY
ENVIRONMENT

VICTIMS

INCIDENCE

MATERIAL DAMAGE

For most Americans, the word *drought* conjures up dusty images from John Steinbeck's novel *The Grapes of Wrath*—or director John Ford's film adaptation of that novel—in which caravans of impoverished Okies, their meager possessions piled atop battered old cars and trucks, embarked on an exodus to California during the Great Depression. They were fleeing one of the worst droughts the United States has ever known, which had turned the once-verdant Great Plains region into an arid, inhospitable dust bowl.

Drought

Europe's worst drought occurred in 1921–22 in southern Russia and the Ukraine, the agricultural breadbasket of the former Soviet Union. The ensuing famine took about 5 million lives. Devastating as they sound, these droughts were mild compared to the apocalyptic lack of water that has tormented Africa for almost 20 years. Since 1973, a severe drought has parched the continent, causing famine and disease. Millions of Africans have died.

It was during the late 1960s that meteorologists began to notice that the Sahara Desert was creeping southward into the Sahel, the semidry region on the southern fringe of the Sahara that includes Mauritania, Mali, Niger, Chad, the Sudan, and parts of Ethiopia. With the encroaching sands came drought conditions. The 20 million inhabitants of the Sahel watched helplessly as the drought destroyed their pasturelands and crops, dried up their wells and rivers, and killed a third of their cattle and over 100,000 people. It was feared that as many as 6 million people might die, until over a million tons of food were donated by other nations. But a decade later, the drought brought another famine, and today, as the drought continues, the Sahel is in the grips of what the Save the Children Foundation calls "the worst famine in Africa in living memory." Twenty-nine million people face starvation.

Name/Description

The word *drought* is from the Anglo-Saxon *dryge*, meaning "dry." A drought is a prolonged lack or insufficiency of rain in a certain area or region. (The longest known rainless period occurred in Chile's Atacama Desert and lasted 400 years.) There are four basic types of drought. A permanent drought characterizes the driest climates, where agriculture is impossible without continuous irrigation. Seasonal droughts occur in areas with well-defined rainy and dry seasons. In these areas crops are planted accordingly. Unpredictable droughts involve an abnormal or unexpected rainfall failure and can occur almost anywhere. These droughts often affect only small areas.

Droughts have killed more people than any other single natural disaster.

Invisible droughts usually occur when high temperatures cause high rates of evaporation that even frequent rains cannot compensate for.

Injury/Illness/Trauma

Droughts cause famines, which in turn cause malnutrition and starvation. Disease is also a threat: inhabitants of drought-stricken areas are often forced to use contaminated water sources. (See Injury/Illness/Trauma, page 104.)

Drought

Material Damage

Droughts pose the most serious threat to agriculture in the world. In the United States, a 1983 drought caused $10 billion worth of damage to crops.

Prevention

Efforts have been made to prevent or relieve droughts by seeding clouds to induce precipitation, but they have had limited success. Drought warnings must be taken seriously. Warnings concerning the Sahel disaster were largely ignored by African and Western governments until it was too late. And in drought-stricken nations, priorities need to be changed. Many droughts occur in overpopulated countries where civil strife and war are rampant. Money and manpower are spent on procuring and using arms instead of initiating desperately needed irrigation and agricultural projects. The situation in the Sudan provides a good example. The Sudan could feed itself, and even export food; less than half of its arable lands are being cultivated. Instead, the Sudanese government is spending $1 million a day fighting a destructive civil war.

DUST DEVIL

INJURY/ILLNESS/
TRAUMA

CLIMATE

PRIMARY
ENVIRONMENT

VICTIMS

INCIDENCE

MATERIAL DAMAGE

"One could see them," recalled Loren Eiseley, "hesitantly stalking across the alkali flats on a hot day, debating perhaps in their tall, rotating columns, whether to ascend and assume more formidable shapes. They were the trickster part of an otherwise pedestrian landscape." Eiseley was remembering the dust devils he often saw during his childhood years in Nebraska. Every summer, hundreds of thousands of these devilish whirlwinds dance across the arid and semiarid regions of the world. During a scientific census of dust devils undertaken near Tucson, Arizona, from June 23 to July 28, 1963, a total of 1,663 dust devils were spotted, a daily average of 46.

Dust Devil

Dust devils are referred to by many different names; in California, they are called sand augers; in France, trombes giratoires (gyrating spouts); in Japan, dragon twists; and in the Sahara, waltzing jinns (genies).

Name/Description

Dust devil is just one of many common names for the small, brief whirlwinds that frequently occur in flat, dry, hot areas (although they also occasionally appear in more temperate climates). In California, they are called sand augers; in France, *trombes giratoires* (gyrating spouts); in Japan, dragon twists; and in the Sahara, waltzing jinn (genies).

Dust devils assist in the distribution of heat in the atmosphere. Unlike tornadoes, dust devils develop from the ground upward and operate independently of clouds, usually appearing against cloudless skies. A large, hot, flat surface, such as the desert floor, results in an unstable layer of air close to the ground. This air tries to rise, but because the whole surface layer cannot rise at once, small, individual cells form and rise. A gentle breeze provides a twist to these rising air cells, which then ascend in a rapid spiral, collecting dust and other debris. The shape of a dust devil is usually that of a cylindrical column or a cone, and they are often tilted forward "as if anxious to reach their destination." They travel at about 10 miles per hour; they can be from a few inches to several hundred feet wide; and they can reach a height of about 300 feet. Most dust devils are short-lived, and they sometimes appear in lines or groups like desert caravans.

Injury/Illness/Trauma

Dust devils rarely cause serious injuries. However, the blowing dust and sand can irritate the eyes and cause eye infections and can also cause respiratory problems, especially for people with allergies or other respiratory ailments.

Material Damage

A dust devil can lift a jackrabbit into the air and harm small livestock. In the southwestern United States, dust devils have overturned cars. Windblown sand is highly abrasive and can scrape glass, blast away paint, and wear away wood and plaster.

Prevention

In areas where dust devils are frequent, exposed surfaces can be specially treated to reduce abrasion damage.

Survival

- If a dust devil heads your way, go indoors. If you are caught out in the open, cover your eyes, nose, and mouth until the dust devil passes. A surgical mask is helpful in any desertlike environment.

EARTHQUAKE

INJURY/ILLNESS/
TRAUMA

CLIMATE

PRIMARY
ENVIRONMENT

VICTIMS

INCIDENCE

MATERIAL DAMAGE

No other natural phenomenon is as destructive over so large an area in so short a time as an earthquake. The earthquake that struck the Shensi province of China in 1556 lasted only minutes but killed approximately 830,000 people and destroyed entire towns and villages. The famous San Francisco earthquake at the turn of the century devastated four square miles of the city, claimed 700 lives, and left 250,000 people homeless. Following the quake, a fire raged for three days before it was extinguished by rain. A powerful predawn earthquake in Guatemala City in 1976 buried sleeping citizens in their adobe houses. Twenty–three thousand were killed, another 50,000 injured, and 1 million were left homeless.

Dangerous Natural Phenomena

Perhaps the most terrifying aspect of an earthquake is that it strikes so violently with so little warning. *Life* magazine photographer Carl Mydans described his experience in the 1948 earthquake in Fukui, Japan, which demolished the town and left 3,500 dead. "I was sitting at dinner," Mydans recalled, "Suddenly, with no warning, the floor pushed up under us and chunks of concrete from the walls and ceiling began crashing about us. Someone shouted 'Earthquake,' but that was unnecessary. We were already rushing for the door . . . struggling to keep our balance, as tables toppled, dishes smashed. . . . I was uplifted from my feet and tossed sharply aside and smacked into the wall. . . . A moment's silence, then little voices of human beings—shouts, cries, rose in a din throughout the city."

Name/Description

Most earthquakes are caused by seismic waves, or shock waves, generated by disturbances in the earth's crust (some quakes are caused by volcanic activity). Although there are probably 1 million quakes annually (mostly below the sea), only about 3,000 of them affect the earth's surface in a noticeable way.

The earth is encased by a shell of rock, which is divided like a jigsaw puzzle into more than a dozen massive, interlocking plates called tectonic plates. Ranging in thickness from 5 to 70 miles, they float on the earth's semimolten mantle, which surrounds the earth's core. When the plates' edges grind and scrape against one another, tremendous energy is released in the form of seismic waves, which cause earthquakes.

The site of the tectonic disturbance is known as the epicenter. The first wave to emanate from the epicenter, called P for primary, travels at a speed of a few miles per second. The S, or secondary wave, moves at a little over half the speed of the P wave. Often called Push and Shake, these initial waves may be followed by others known as aftershocks. Earthquakes can affect huge areas and are often followed by fires and storm surges.

Earthquake

There are approximately 1 million earthquakes annually, yet only 3,000 of these noticeably affect the earth's surface.

Injury/Illness/Trauma

Earthquakes kill approximately 15,000 people annually. In severe quakes, most victims are killed by falling debris. Many are wounded and trapped under collapsed structures, where they may die from their wounds, from exposure, or from suffocation. Others are killed in the fires and floods that often follow major quakes. Starvation and disease can also become factors in stricken areas. (See Injury/Illness/Trauma, page 104.)

Dangerous Natural Phenomena

Material Damage

Earthquakes are catastrophic; they destroy buildings, wreck bridges, crack dams, break power and water lines, start fires, and ruin roadways and train tracks. In Anchorage, Alaska, in 1964, an earthquake destroyed 75 percent of the state's industrial capacity. As with so many disasters, material damage is always worse in underdeveloped nations, where many structures are poorly built.

Prevention

The U.S. Geological Survey's National Earthquake Information Service monitors seismic activity from 3,000 stations in 125 countries. Seismologists can predict possible earthquake locations but not the time when the quake will occur. Animals such as dogs, seagulls, snakes, cats, rats, and horses are capable of detecting smaller vibrations than humans can feel, and their behavior can indicate impending earthquakes. Dr. Frank Press of the Massachusetts Institute of Technology has stated that "animal behavior as a means of predicting earthquakes must now be taken very seriously." In earthquake-prone areas, especially in the Third and Fourth Worlds, improvements in the building of quake-proof structures are needed. In the Mexico City earthquake of 1985, many supposedly earthquake-resistant buildings crumbled.

Survival

- If you are indoors when an earthquake hits, get under something that will protect you from falling debris.
- Wait until the first tremors stop and then get out to open ground.
- If you are at home, turn off the gas and electricity before leaving.
- If you are outside when a quake hits, get away from tall buildings and other structures.

EL NIÑO

INJURY/ILLNESS/
TRAUMA

CLIMATE

PRIMARY
ENVIRONMENT

VICTIMS

INCIDENCE

MATERIAL DAMAGE

About once every decade at Christmastime, *El Niño* (The Child), an abnormally warm ocean current, comes to the western coast of South America. To the casual traveler, the unexpected arrival of *El Niño* might seem like a lovely Christmas present; the weather turns tropical, and the cool ocean becomes warm. But for the native inhabitants of Ecuador and Peru, the arrival of *El Niño* is no cause for celebration.

Dangerous Natural Phenomena

Since World War II, there have been eight major *El Niño* events; the worst of these was *El Niño* of 1982–83, which wreaked havoc on agriculture and the fishing industries of Ecuador and Peru. In the overly warm, nutrient-poor waters of *El Niño*, plankton could not survive. Plankton is the primary food source for the fish of those waters, and thus the fish could not survive either. The effect on the local fishing industry was devastating. Agriculture was also affected; many of the crops grown in Peru and Ecuador depend for fertilization on birds that feed on plankton and fish. When their source of food disappeared, so did the birds, and crop yields declined dramatically.

The meteorological impact of *El Niño* was also dramatic. Ecuador and Peru were hit by heavy rains, which caused floods, mud slides, and landslides. Railways and highways on the steep slopes of the Andes Mountains were swept away or shut down. Drinking water was contaminated and there were outbreaks of typhoid and other diseases. In Ecuador, a state of emergency was declared.

The influence of *El Niño* was felt elsewhere as well; the great volumes of overly warm water off the coast of South America disrupted global weather patterns. In Australia and India there were droughts that resulted in runaway brush fires and monstrous dust storms, which were eventually followed by rains that caused floods of "Old Testament proportions." The West Coast of the United States was ravaged by storms that then moved southeast across the country, causing floods that forced the evacuation of thousands. The East Coast experienced record-breaking snowfalls and, in some areas, the wettest spring in recent memory.

Name/Description

The phrase *El Niño* refers to the Christ Child, who arrived at Christmas, as *El Niño* does. *El Niño* is believed to be caused by unusually weak trade winds, which result in high sea-surface temperatures in the tropical Pacific Ocean. This in turn prevents the usual upswelling of volumes of deep, cold, plankton-rich water off the west coast of South America. The

34

El Niño

El Niño has resulted in floods, mud slides, and landslides.

absence of the cold water results in the dominant tropical current known as *El Niño* and the associated phenomena.

Injury/Illness/Trauma

El Niño brings heavy rains, which in turn cause landslides (see Landslide, page 56), mud slides (see Mud Slide, page 68), and floods (see River Flooding, page 72). *El Niño* is also associated with drought (see Drought, page 22) and failure of major food–source production, resulting in widespread malnutrition, starvation, and disease.

Dangerous Natural Phenomena

Material Damage

Long–term material damage associated with *El Niño* on a worldwide scale is incalculable.

Prevention

In 1985 the Tropical Ocean and Global Atmosphere (TOGA) project began. TOGA is an international effort to better understand *El Niño*, its causes, and its effects on global weather patterns. An army of oceanographers and meteorologists, equipped with three environmental satellites and an armada of vessels, are participating in the project. The ultimate goal of TOGA is to learn how to predict severe occurrences of *El Niño* in order to be better prepared for them.

FOG

INJURY/ILLNESS/
TRAUMA

CLIMATE

PRIMARY
ENVIRONMENT

VICTIMS

INCIDENCE

MATERIAL DAMAGE

Some of the worst maritime disasters in history were caused by fog. One of the foggiest—and most hazardous—stretches of water in the world is found off the Grand Banks of Newfoundland in summer, when warm Gulf Stream winds blow over the cold Labrador Current. The great, gray fogbanks that are formed conceal potentially deadly icebergs that drift down from the north.

The Atlantic coast of the United States has seen its share of foggy maritime disasters. In 1952, the oil tankers *Esso Suez* and *Esso Greensboro* collided in dense fog 200 miles south of Morgan City, Louisiana. The *Esso Greensboro* was fully loaded and burst into flames. Only five crew members survived. In 1956, the *Andrea Doria* and the *Stockholm* collided in thick fog off the coast of Massachusetts. Fifty–one people were killed. Fog has also been implicated in airline tragedies. In March 1977 a dense fog proved fatal to 582 people when two jumbo jets collided on an airport runway at Tenerife, in the Canary Islands.

But fog is not always unwelcome. During World War II, fog probably saved thousands of lives during the famous evacuation of Dunkirk, France. Belgium's surrender to Germany in 1940 left thousands of Allied troops stranded on mainland Europe, badly outnumbered and out-gunned by the Nazi war machine. British troops and members of the Free French fought their way across northern France to the port city of Dunkirk on the English Channel. Trapped and exposed on the beach, the Allied troops waited to be pounded mercilessly by the German Luftwaffe. Miraculously, a heavy fog rolled in, obscuring the soldiers on the beach and allowing them to be evacuated by a heroic, makeshift flotilla of mostly civilian vessels that ferried them across the channel to safety in England.

Name/Description

The word *fog* is probably of Scandinavian origin, evolving from the Norse *fjog* or *fjug*, meaning a thin layer of cloud. Fog is created when warm, moist air is cooled to the point that it cannot hold moisture any longer. The moisture is squeezed out in the form of droplets so fine and buoyant that they become suspended and drift easily, forming fog. The only difference between fog and clouds is that fog stays close to the ground.

Fogs vary greatly in size and duration. A fog may be only a few yards wide and deep, hovering over a small area such as a pond, or it may stretch for hundreds of miles along a coast and be deep enough for a

Fog

**Fog may cover only a small area, or it can stretch
for hundreds of miles.**

ship to become lost within it for days on end. Some fogs last only one
night, whereas others may last several days or even weeks. Fogs tend to
perpetuate themselves by shutting out the sun's rays, thus preventing
the ground and air from becoming warm enough to burn off the fog.

Injury/Illness/Trauma

Heavy fog can reduce visibility to a few feet or less, causing vehicular
accidents on land, at sea, and in the air. Devastating chain-reaction

collisions on roads and highways, involving hundreds of cars and trucks and causing serious injuries and even deaths, are often attributed to fog. (See Injury/Illness/Trauma, page 104.)

Material Damage

Fog can be extremely costly. Along with the many accidents caused by fog, disruption of transport is a frequent problem. The shipping and trucking industries are seemingly at the mercy of fog. And in the United States alone, airports are closed for more than 100 hours annually because of fog; takeoffs and landings are usually not permitted if visibility is less than 984 feet (300 meters).

Prevention

During World War II, when fog hampered the landings of the Royal Air Force aircraft, England developed a method for lifting fogs on short notice. Rows of oil-burning jet faucets were arranged around airfields. The heat from the faucets could raise fogs, pushing them as high as 100 feet in minutes. Over 2,500 aircraft landings were assisted in this manner. After the war, this method was abandoned because of its high operational costs.

Today, chemicals that impair fog formation are spread over swamps and lakes in the vicinity of airports and highways. Certain fogs can be seeded with dry ice or liquid propane particles that cause the fog droplets to freeze and fall. And improved radar techniques have greatly reduced nautical and air accidents caused by fog.

GLACIER

INJURY/ILLNESS/
TRAUMA

CLIMATE

PRIMARY
ENVIRONMENT

VICTIMS

INCIDENCE

MATERIAL DAMAGE

Perhaps it is the primeval beauty of glaciers that has drawn so many climbers and adventurers to risk their lives on them. In 1892, Martin Conway, a pioneer explorer and climber of the Himalaya Mountains, described the cold solitude and eerie beauty of the Hispar Glacier. "There was no sign of animal life," wrote Conway. "Nowhere was there a bright patch of sunshine. . . . The vast snowfields beyond were all a pallid grey like the sky. Nothing glittered. Silence was only broken by a faint hum of moving waters. . . . All appeared still as death, and I sat motionless an hour or more and felt as though time had ceased."

Glaciers are attractive to climbers and explorers, but they are also unforgiving. One summer on Oregon's Mount Hood, 17 climbers labored up the face of a glacier. Near the summit, one climber slipped and dragged the other 16 climbers down with him into a crevasse. They tumbled down on top of one another, a tangle of boots, rope, packs, and other climbing gear. Luckily, nobody was killed, although all the climbers were cut, bruised, and badly shaken.

One member of a climbing expedition led by the famous English mountaineer Chris Bonington was not so fortunate. During a 1985 traversal of a glacier on the Ogre, a 23,413-foot peak in the Karakoram Range of Pakistan, Bonington lost Don Morrison, a member of his expedition, down a crevasse. Morrison was killed. Bonington's subsequent descent was harrowing. "It would be all too easy to step through the snow cover into a hidden crevasse," Bonington wrote. "As I plodded along in the glimmer of dawn back towards the Ogre, each step was filled with trepidation. I constantly glanced around me, trying to glimpse hints of hidden crevasses indicated by slight creases in the dim grey snow. At times the crust would give, my foot would plunge, and I'd experience a stab of terror."

Name/Description

The word *glacier* comes from the Latin *glacies*, meaning "frost." A glacier is a large mass of mobile, permanent ice formed by the consolidation and recrystallization of snow. It is the movement of glaciers that distinguishes them from snow fields or ice fields. Glaciers creep slowly downhill—most move about three feet a day—into valleys, onto plains, or into oceans. Glaciers are found in all of the major mountain ranges of the world and on every continent except Australia. Glaciers can be hundreds and even thousands of miles long and wide, and thousands of feet thick. Almost 75 percent of the earth's fresh water is stored in glaciers.

Crevasses are fissures or cracks in glaciers that are caused by the stress produced by the movement of the glacier. Crevasses can be up to 65 feet wide, 150 feet deep, and several hundred yards long. Often covered by a thin layer of snow or ice that hides them, crevasses pose a threat to climbers and skiers.

Icefalls are another hazard associated with glaciers. An icefall is a chaotic, perilous area strewn with tottering blocks of ice—some as big as

Glacier

Glaciers may be thousands of miles long and wide, and thousands of feet thick.

houses—and riddled with jagged outcroppings and pinnacles of ice jutting up among the crevasses. The blocks of ice, called seracs, are dangerously unstable and may come tumbling down at any time.

Injury/Illness/Trauma

On glaciers, most fatalities occur when climbers or skiers fall into crevasses and die from injury or exposure. A crevasse provides an icy and usually permanent tomb. Sometimes, however, after it has moved sufficiently, a glacier may regurgitate a body. The frozen corpses of two 19th-century climbers who had fallen into a crevasse in a European glacier reappeared 42 years later. Most other glacier fatalities, especially in the Himalayas, are caused by falling seracs. (See Injury/Illness/Trauma, page 104.)

Material Damage

At the present time, glaciers pose no real threat to any permanent cities, towns, or structures. However, a dramatic change in the earth's weather patterns could have a catastrophic effect on glaciers. A serious drop in temperature could precipitate another ice age, during which the glaciers would expand and swallow up anything in their path. During the last ice age, which occurred about 18,000 years ago, glaciers covered one-third of the planet's surface. A sharp rise in temperature, on the other hand, might cause the glaciers at the earth's poles to melt, which in turn would cause sea levels around the world to rise by as much as 200 feet. The ensuing flooding of coastal areas would be disastrous.

Prevention

Scientists now fear that unchecked global warming, caused primarily by an excess of carbon dioxide in the atmosphere, could eventually cause the polar ice caps and glaciers to melt. Governments around the world are attempting to reduce the industrial emission of carbon dioxide to prevent such a crisis.

Survival

- Glaciers should be crossed in the middle, where there are fewest crevasses, and at dawn, when snow and ice bridges over crevasses are most solid.

- Check for concealed crevasses by jabbing through the snow with a long-handled ice pick or a similar object. If it breaks through to open air, turn back.

- At least three people should be tied together during the crossing of a glacier; it will take at least two people to extract someone from a crevasse.

HAIL

INJURY/ILLNESS/
TRAUMA

CLIMATE

PRIMARY
ENVIRONMENT

VICTIMS

INCIDENCE

MATERIAL DAMAGE

Veteran airline pilot Robert Black described what it is like to fly through a hailstorm: "Flying through hail is probably the most nerve-racking experience in the sky. The clatter is overpowering. Some hailstones are bigger than tennis balls and thousands of these . . . can damage an aircraft badly." A hailstorm is no less threatening to the earthbound. During a 15-minute hailstone deluge near Kemptville, Canada, on June 26, 1952, an estimated 5,000 windows were broken, 500 dogs, cats, and fowl were killed, 200 cars were severely damaged, almost 100 roofs were punctured, and 15 acres of crops were ruined. On July 14, 1953, a 600-pound hog was battered to death when it was caught out in the open during a violent hailstorm in Alberta, Canada.

Hail can be deadly for humans, also. On April 30, 1888, 246 people were killed by hailstones "as large as cricket balls" (about the size of a baseball) during a sudden storm over Moradabad, Uttar Pradesh, India. Two hundred people died in a two-hour hailstorm in the Hunan province of China on June 19, 1932.

Hailstorms sometimes carry "stowaways" along with them. There are numerous reports of living creatures, such as frogs and turtles, descending with the hailstones, presumably having been swept into the air by powerful updrafts. According to J. R. Norman, a British ichthyologist, a hailstone as large as a hen's egg fell during a heavy storm over Essen, Germany. Inside the big hailstone was a carp. Charles F. Brooks stated that during a hailstorm in Worcester, Massachusetts, "there was a fall of iced ducks." The ducks had probably been frozen as they flew through the storm.

Name/Description

The word *hail* comes from the Middle English *hægl*. Hail is a shower of balls or clumps of ice known as hailstones, which have been tossed up and down by strong vertical winds in cumulonimbus clouds, acquiring repeated coatings of ice until they grew heavy enough to fall to earth. Hailstones usually have alternating layers of clear and opaque ice. A single hailstone can have as many as 25 layers. Hail typically falls in heavy but localized showers within the area of a thunderstorm (see Thunderstorm, page 84). The largest and heaviest unit of precipitation, hail can fall at speeds of up to 140 miles per hour.

Hailstones can be quite large. Stones over half a foot in diameter and almost a foot and a half in circumference have been recorded. The most damaging hailstones are the rock hard, walnut-sized stones that fall thick and fast in sudden, violent showers, often driven by powerful gusts of wind.

One of the most hail-prone areas in the world is the Nandi Hills of Kenya, Africa, where hail falls approximately 132 days per year. In North

Hail

Hailstones over half a foot in diameter and almost a foot and a half in circumference have been recorded.

America, hail falls most frequently in so–called Hail Alley, a great swath of land that stretches from Texas to Montana, and from the foothills of the Rockies to the Mississippi River. Hail insurance is a necessity for the many farmers of Hail Alley.

Injury/Illness/Trauma

Hailstones can inflict serious head injuries, knock victims unconscious, and even kill them. (See Injury/Illness/Trauma, page 104.)

Dangerous Natural Phenomena

Material Damage

In the United States, hail causes more than $500 million in damage annually. Wheat and corn farmers bear the brunt of it. Hail can strip the leaves and ears off cornstalks and flatten wheat fields. It can also bruise melons, puncture tomatoes, shred tobacco leaves—in North Carolina annual tobacco crop losses caused by hail exceed $3 million—knock down grape arbors, and destroy flowers. Hail can injure and even kill livestock as well as domestic animals. Hailstones also batter houses and vehicles. Hail has damaged and endangered aircraft flying as high as 45,000 feet.

Prevention

Ground radar can sometimes detect hail in an approaching storm. Radar mounted on aircraft can detect hail within a 20-mile radius. The Severe Storm Warning Center in Kansas City, Missouri, carries regular hail-warning forecasts. Following such a warning, windows, skylights, and vehicles can be protected by covering them with heavy tarpaulins. Protecting crops from hail is more difficult. In Italy, scaffolding is erected over certain crops, such as oranges, and when a hailstorm starts, heavy matting is pulled across the scaffolding.

In agricultural areas of the Commonwealth of Independent States, various cloud-seeding methods have been investigated. In one experiment, anti-aircraft batteries fired special shells into threatening clouds. When the shells burst, they released chemical agents into the clouds, causing precipitation to fall in the form of rain or tiny ice crystals rather than hail. Similar experiments have been done in the United States, with inconclusive results.

Survival

• If a hailstorm comes your way, take cover.

HURRICANE

INJURY/ILLNESS/
TRAUMA

CLIMATE

PRIMARY
ENVIRONMENT

VICTIMS

INCIDENCE

MATERIAL DAMAGE

"Do you know that you cannot breathe with a hurricane blowing full in your face?" asks yachtsman Weston Martyr. "You cannot see either; the impact on your eyeballs of spray and rain flying at over 100 miles per hour makes seeing quite impossible. You hear nothing except the scream and booming of the wind. . . . You cannot even crawl." Martyr survived his encounter with a hurricane, but these ferocious storms have killed more than 45,000 people in the 20th century.

In August 1992, the costliest hurricane in American history struck the Bahamas, Florida, and Louisiana; an estimated $15 billion to $20 billion in damage was incurred in Florida alone, making Hurricane Andrew the most expensive natural disaster ever! It was later downgraded to a tropical storm, but not before claiming 20 lives. "It sounded like two trains crashing," said Marsha Rouchon, who had taken shelter in a Florida high school gymnasium to wait out the hurricane. Wind speeds reached over 140 miles per hour, resulting in the destruction of 63,000 homes in Florida, and leaving 250,000 Floridians homeless.

Name/Description

The word *hurricane* is derived from the word *hurakían*, which was the name the Taino Indians of the Greater Antilles and the Bahamas gave to their storm god. A hurricane is a massive—up to 400 miles in radius—and violent cyclonic weather system that begins as a tropical depression and gains strength from warm water and moist, warm air. A tropical depression is officially classified as a hurricane when its winds surpass 74 miles per hour. Hurricanes spawn tornadoes and monstrous storm clouds and have a central core where the "eye" of the storm—an area of calm—is located. Most hurricanes travel on a westerly course, but they are notoriously unpredictable and erratic. The average life span of a hurricane is nine days, during which it may travel over 3,000 miles.

Hurricanes—and typhoons, their cousins in the South Pacific—are the most powerful of storms. It is hard to accurately measure full-force hurricane winds because the wind meters usually break under the strain. Sustained hurricane wind speeds are usually estimated to be about 100 miles per hour, with gusts of up to 225 miles per hour. The volume of rain unleashed by a hurricane is prodigious.

Injury/Illness/Trauma

During hurricanes, many people drown in the accompanying floods. Others are killed by wind-driven debris or crushed beneath falling

Up to 100 times larger than a thunderstorm and 1,000 times more powerful than a tornado, a hurricane is without meteorological peer.

objects. Food shortages and disease from contaminated water supplies often occur in the wake of a hurricane. (See Injury/Illness/Trauma, page 104.)

Material Damage

Hurricanes can be as costly as earthquakes and volcanic eruptions. Rough seas capsize boats and destroy offshore oil rigs, while high winds topple trees and telephone poles, tear down power lines, send roofs and shutters flying, and hurl heavy debris against structures and through windows. The worst damage, however, is caused by flooding, which destroys homes and erodes beaches and coastlines.

Prevention

The National Oceanic and Atmospheric Administration has experimented with seeding techniques to try to reduce the force of hurricanes. Called Project Stormfury, this effort involved flying an airplane into a hurricane and seeding the storm clouds around the eye with silver iodide in order to form a larger eye, which would reduce wind speeds. Although Project Stormfury had some success—Hurricane Debbie's winds were reduced by 30 percent in 1969—early warning, preparation, and evacuation are still the soundest methods of preventing damage, injury, and loss of life during a hurricane.

Survival

- If you know a hurricane is coming, bring in or tie down outside furniture.
- Board up or tape windows.
- If you are caught in the house, shut off the electricity and gas and stay away from windows.
- If you live in a flood area, evacuate as quickly as possible. (See Disaster Preparation and Survival, page 106.)

ICEBERG

INJURY/ILLNESS/
TRAUMA

CLIMATE

PRIMARY
ENVIRONMENT

VICTIMS

INCIDENCE

MATERIAL DAMAGE

Just before midnight on April 14, 1912, the 46,000-ton luxury liner *Titanic* smashed into an iceberg 95 miles south of Newfoundland. The *Titanic*, the largest ship in the world at the time, was on its maiden voyage from Liverpool to New York City, but it would never arrive at its destination. Within two hours of its collision with the iceberg, the "unsinkable" *Titanic* had disappeared beneath the frigid waters of the Atlantic along with more than 1,500 passengers and crew. The *Californian*, the only vessel in the vicinity, made no attempt to aid the *Titanic*; its radio operator had gone off duty and thus none of the frantic distress calls issued from the doomed ocean liner were received. It was one of the worst peacetime disasters in maritime history.

On January 30, 1959, the Danish passenger–cargo ship *Hans Hedtoft* collided with an iceberg off the southern tip of Greenland. Like the *Titanic*, the *Hans Hedtoft* was on its maiden voyage, and like the *Titanic*, it was considered unsinkable. But despite its reinforced steel hull and its armored bow and stern, the *Hans Hedtoft* received a death blow from the iceberg. Ships and aircraft in the area picked up radio transmissions from the stricken vessel and hurried to the location they were given. But when the would–be rescuers got there, they saw no sign of the *Hans Hedtoft*. The search continued for days, but no trace of the ship or its passengers and crew was ever found.

Name/Description

The English word *iceberg* comes from the Danish or Norwegian *isberg*, meaning "ice mountain." And icebergs are indeed mountains of ice. Mariners and aviators have reported seeing icebergs that were 30 to 40 miles long and that rose thousands of feet above the water. An Antarctic iceberg "about the size of Belgium" was once sighted in the Pacific Ocean. Usually, only about one-tenth of an iceberg's total bulk is visible above the surface of the water, so the true size of these monsters can only be estimated.

Most icebergs—about 7,500 annually—are calved from glaciers along the coast of Greenland. These Arctic icebergs are smaller but much more numerous than their massive Antarctic cousins. They occur in an endless variety of abstract shapes. Antarctic icebergs are typically flat-topped masses that have broken off the Antarctic ice cap, which juts out over the ocean like a gigantic tabletop. Often these huge glacial fragments break off and float away with colonies of hapless penguins aboard. An iceberg may drift for years and cover thousands of miles on its journey before it becomes stranded in shallow waters, freezes fast to a landmass, or melts in warm waters.

Injury/Illness/Trauma

Humans cannot survive long in icy waters. Death by drowning is the usual fate of people who have been forced into the water after a collision with an iceberg. Survivors adrift in lifeboats may suffer from exposure and hypothermia. (See Injury/Illness/Trauma, page 104.)

Iceberg

Mariners and aviators have spotted icebergs 30 to 40 miles long
that rose thousands of feet above the water.

Material Damage

Icebergs have sunk or damaged innumerable vessels. They are most dangerous to vessels plying the North Atlantic shipping lanes in the spring, but they have been sighted as far south as Bermuda.

Prevention

Usually, 90 percent of an iceberg is underwater, which makes it hard to see until it is too late. The International Ice Patrol was founded after the *Titanic* disaster. Financed by 20 nations, it is run by the United States Coast Guard. Aircraft, ships, and satellites are used to detect icebergs. Once an iceberg has been located, wind and ocean current information is used to predict the iceberg's drift. Researchers are still searching for an effective method of melting or destroying icebergs that drift into shipping lanes.

LANDSLIDE

INJURY/ILLNESS/
TRAUMA

CLIMATE

PRIMARY
ENVIRONMENT

VICTIMS

INCIDENCE

MATERIAL DAMAGE

The statistics of the prehistoric landslide in the Saidmarreh Valley in Iran are staggering. A slab of limestone, nine miles long by three miles wide and weighing 50 billion tons, rumbled down into the valley, gaining so much momentum that it slid for miles across the valley floor and roared up the other side, climbing up and over a 1,500–foot–high ridge. For-tunately, the Saidmarreh Valley was uninhabited at the time.

The town of Plurs, Switzerland, was not so fortunate. In 1618, nearly half the side of a mountain fell and obliterated Plurs. Of a population of some 1,500 only 4 were left; and they were away at the time. In 1903, 1,000 cubic feet of limestone crashed down the slopes of Turtle Mountain

Landslide

in Alberta, Canada. Like a great wave, the mass of limestone roared across the valley floor at more than 100 miles per hour and surged 400 feet up the opposite mountainside before stopping. The landslide claimed over a mile of the Canadian Pacific Railway, several houses, and 76 victims.

In August 1950, near West Yellowstone, Montana, an earthquake triggered a landslide in Madison Canyon. Twenty campers were engulfed; the remains of some of the victims were never recovered. The landslide carried an automobile for seven miles before it was smashed against a row of trees. From 1978 to 1988, there were more than 4,000 landslides in the Los Angeles basin of California, where they are still a regular occurrence.

Name/Description

A landslide is the rapid and often violent mass movement of rock, earth, or artificial landfill down a slope or incline. Landslides can be triggered by the effects of erosion from heavy rains, or by vibrations caused by explosions, earthquakes, or even the passage of traffic near an unstable mass.

Injury/Illness/Trauma

Most landslide victims are killed outright or die within a short period of time from suffocation, bodily injury, or shock. Others may survive the landslide itself only to succumb to exposure or hypothermia while awaiting rescue. Injuries caused by landslides include broken bones, sprains, and lacerations. (See Injury/Illness/Trauma, page 104.)

Material Damage

Landslides obliterate anything in their path. In the United States they pose a major economic threat, causing $1 billion worth of damage annually.

Landslides often act as waves, roaring down a mountain, across a valley, and over the opposite mountainside before stopping.

Prevention

Potential landslide areas must be recognized and clearly marked. Areas with old slide debris are clearly visible in aerial photographs. The strength and stability of soils can be determined by laboratory testing. Once a potential landslide area has been discovered, it can be stabilized in a variety of ways, including water drainage and the injection of grout or chemicals that strengthen clay cohesion.

Landslide

Survival

- If you are hiking in a landslide area, try to stay near the top of hills and ridges and avoid walking through gullies and ravines. If you are in a group, do not follow in each others' tracks; this in itself may help to further destabilize a mass of loose material.

- If you find yourself in the path of a landslide, flatten yourself against the nearest tree or rock wall.

- If you see someone being swept away, try to keep the victim in sight as long as possible in order to locate the victim quickly once the landslide stops.

LIGHTNING

INJURY/ILLNESS/
TRAUMA

CLIMATE

PRIMARY
ENVIRONMENT

VICTIMS

INCIDENCE

MATERIAL DAMAGE

Mention lightning and two old adages spring to mind: "Lightning never strikes the same place twice" and "Don't stand under a tree." The first saying is inaccurate. New York City's Empire State Building has been struck 12 times during a single storm and receives about 23 bolts annually. Park ranger Roy C. Sullivan of Washington State is a human lightning rod, having been struck *seven times* (so far). Sullivan, who is either very lucky or very unlucky, had one of his toenails blasted off by lightning in 1942, had his eyebrows singed in 1969, had his left shoulder scorched in 1970, had his hair set on fire in 1972 and then again in 1973, had his ankle injured in 1976, and suffered burns on his chest and stomach in 1977. After one incident, Sullivan found that all the change in his pockets had been fused together!

Lightning

The second adage—"Don't stand under a tree"—is good advice; 25 percent of lightning fatalities occur under trees, where people often take shelter during storms. Although most victims are hit by direct strikes, many are also injured or killed by fires and explosions set off by lightning. In 1769, an arsenal at Brescia, Italy, was hit by a bolt of lightning. Over 100 tons of gunpowder exploded, killing 3,000 people and destroying much of the city. A similar accident happened in the United States in 1926, when lightning struck the largest ammunition depot in the nation, at Lake Denmark, New Jersey. Even though the depot was outfitted with numerous lightning rods, it was blasted by a bolt during a storm, which set off a massive explosion that destroyed buildings and killed 16 people. Debris from the depot explosion was found 22 miles away.

Name/Description
A lightning bolt is an electrical discharge from one region of charged particles to another region of oppositely charged particles within a cumulonimbus cloud, usually during a thunderstorm. (Lightning has also been known to occur during snowstorms and sandstorms, and inside clouds over erupting volcanoes.) Such clouds are usually positively charged in the upper regions and negatively charged in the lower regions. Lightning may occur within a single cloud, from cloud to cloud, or, as we most commonly think of it, from cloud to ground. A violent thunderstorm may produce cloud-to-ground discharges at a rate of 100 per second. The sudden heating and expansion of the air around a lightning bolt produces shock waves, which are heard as thunder.

Injury/Illness/Trauma
Most lightning fatalities are caused by cardiac arrest or respiratory paralysis brought on by the passage of electricity through the body. About 600 people worldwide are killed by lightning each year. Victims

who are not killed are often burned, thrown violently to the ground, or knocked unconscious, and they frequently report seeing a blinding flash of light and hearing a deafening bang. Many survivors suffer minimal injuries and simply walk away, and most people who survive the initial strike recover fully. (See Injury/Illness/Trauma, page 104.)

Material Damage

Lightning can blast apart trees and buildings. It can melt and fuse metal and plastic, overload transformers, and travel along wires leading to televisions, telephones, radios, computers, and other electrical appliances, ruining them and sometimes causing explosions and fires inside the home. Lightning can also cause blackouts by striking power stations and lines. Commercial aircraft are struck by lightning more than 1,000 times each year, although damage is minimal. Fires started by lightning cause the most material damage; there are thousands of fires annually, resulting in the loss of over $430 million a year in the United States alone.

Prevention

Lightning rods have proved somewhat effective in protecting structures.

Survival

- If you are caught outside during a thunder and lightning storm, *do not take refuge under a tree!*
- Avoid high ground.
- Golfers should drop their clubs and get off the course, baseball players should drop their bats and retire from the field, and people who are fishing should put down their poles and head for shore (poles, bats, and

Lightning

**A violent storm may produce cloud-to-ground
discharges at a rate of 100 per second.**

golf clubs can attract lightning). Swimmers should get out of the water
and beachgoers should get off the beach.

- People caught out in flat, open areas should lie down on the ground.
- Indoors, unplug all electrical appliances, and stay away from windows,
  large metal objects, and fireplaces. The safest place is a cellar.
- Victims of lightning harbor no residual electrical charge; it is perfectly
  safe to touch and help them.

MONSOON

INJURY/ILLNESS/
TRAUMA

CLIMATE

PRIMARY
ENVIRONMENT

VICTIMS

INCIDENCE

MATERIAL DAMAGE

English astronomer Edmund Halley (1656–1742), discoverer of Halley's comet, was one of the first western scientists to recognize the meteorological importance of the monsoon winds. But the monsoons had long been known to commercial and military seamen. In ancient times, the Indian monsoons kept Phoenician and Greek sea explorers from traveling east toward India and China. It was an admiral of Alexander the Great (356–323 B.C.), king of Macedonia, who first discovered how to use the monsoons—instead of struggling against them—to sail from Arabia to India.

Monsoon

To the people of southern Asia, the monsoons were—and still are—a familiar and vital phenomenon. India's predominantly agricultural economy has always depended on the summer monsoons, which produce nearly all of that region's rainfall for the year. The arrival of the monsoon rains is greeted with joy and reverence; they are considered to be a gift from God (or the gods, depending on the religion). And indeed, every summer they burst over the parched land like a blessing of water from above. The first prime minister of India, Jawaharlal Nehru, described the arrival of the monsoon rains over the city of Bombay: "They came with pomp and circumstance and overwhelmed the city with their lavish gift. There was a ferocity in this sudden meeting of the rain–laden clouds with land. The dry land was lashed by the pouring torrents and converted into a temporary sea. Bombay was not static then; it became elemental, dynamic, changing."

But the life–giving monsoons can also bring death. The amount of rainfall produced in a short period of time by the monsoons is tremendous. At Cherrapunji, on the southern side of the Khasi Hills in Meghalaya, India, the average rainfall in a winter month is about 1 inch, while during the monsoons, it is not unusual for up to 100 inches of rain to fall in a month. During the monsoons of 1899, 642 inches of rain fell on that area. Even the driest fields and riverbeds can only retain so much water, and severe flooding is a yearly threat.

Name/Description

The word *monsoon* is derived from the Arabic *mausim*, meaning "season," and was originally used to describe the seasonal winds that blow across the Arabian Sea, although today it commonly refers to both the winds and the heavy rains they bring in the summer. (Monsoons also occur in any region where extreme temperature differences develop between oceans and continents.) The Asian monsoon wind systems blow consistently from one direction for half the year and from the opposite

Monsoons ultimately may cause famine and drought as well as flooding.

direction for the other half; from the northeast in winter and from the southwest in summer. Winter monsoons have a dominant easterly component and a strong tendency to diverge, subside, and cause drought. Summer monsoons have a dominant westerly component and a strong tendency to converge, rise, and produce rain.

Monsoon

In winter, the Asian continent becomes cooler than the Indian Ocean. Cool winds from the northeast blow across the Indian subcontinent, bringing dry weather. In April and May, however, these winds die down and temperatures soar to uncomfortable levels. Within days, cool monsoon winds sweep in from the Indian Ocean; they meet the hot air that hangs over the land, causing a drop in temperature, storms, and the heavy monsoon rains.

Injury/Illness/Trauma

For injuries and illnesses associated with the monsoons, see River Flooding, page 72, and Tsunami, page 92.

Material Damage

See River Flooding, page 72, and Tsunami, page 92.

Prevention

About 50 percent of the earth's population depends on the monsoon winds and the rains they bring. Monsoons that are longer or shorter than usual can have disastrous effects—including famine and drought as well as flooding—on widespread areas. Monsoon meteorology is now recognized as a vitally important science. In 1978, the World Meteorological Organization began their Monsoon Experiment (Monex), in the hopes of learning how to better understand the monsoon phenomenon.

MUD SLIDE

INJURY/ILLNESS/
TRAUMA

CLIMATE

PRIMARY
ENVIRONMENT

VICTIMS

INCIDENCE

MATERIAL DAMAGE

Just before the turn of the century, near Trondheim Fjord, Norway, 70 million cubic tons of wet clay slid into the Verdal Valley, destroying 22 farms and killing 111 people. One lucky family survived after riding the flow for nearly four hours on the roof of a farmhouse! In 1920, in China's Kansu province, a series of catastrophic mud slides (also known as mudflows) set off by an earthquake buried an estimated 100,000 people.

One of the most infamous mud slides in modern times occurred in October 1966 in Aberfan, Wales. Heavy autumn rains sent a 500,000-ton

Mud Slide

mountain of mining waste sliding down upon the little town. One hundred and forty-four people were killed; 116 of the dead were children trapped in a doomed schoolhouse. In spite of repeated warnings that the waste pile was getting dangerously high and unstable—debris had been heaped on it for over 50 years—no effort had been made to remove or reduce it.

For the inhabitants of the *favelas*, or hillside slums, of Rio de Janeiro, Brazil, mud slides are an annual nightmare. They usually occur during the rainy season, burying hundreds or even thousands of little shacks and many of their inhabitants under tons of mud and garbage. In January 1988, after 18 inches of rain fell on the city, 277 Brazilians were killed, 1,000 were injured, and 18,500 were left homeless by devastating mud slides. Rio de Janeiro's mayor, Roberto Saturnino Braga, remarked that the city looked like it had been "destroyed by a giant."

Name/Description

A mud slide or mudflow is a moving mass of soil and/or debris usually set in motion by heavy rains or melting snow. The most common type of mud slide occurs in arid, mountainous regions, when sudden, heavy rains wash vast quantities of loose soil, clay, and rock down steep mountain slopes into gulleys, ravines, and valleys. As the muddy mass moves downhill, water is lost by seepage while more solid matter is collected, ultimately giving the mudflow the consistency of ready-mix concrete. Mud slides like these may appear with little warning, often with a steep, wall-like front, and spread over everything in their path.

In places such as Rio de Janeiro or Aberfan, mud slides are often compounded by large deposits of refuse or industrial debris of one kind or another. Another type of mud slide occurs on the slopes of an active volcano when torrential rains saturate heaps of freshly fallen volcanic ash. Geologists use the Japanese word *lahar* to describe volcanic mudflows.

After a devastating mud slide hit Rio de Janeiro in 1988, the mayor remarked, "It's as if the city had been destroyed by a giant."

Injury/Illness/Trauma

Mudflows can cause many of the same injuries associated with land-slides (see Landslide, page 56). The acidic volcanic mud in a lahar poses an additional threat; it can strip clothes and even skin off people.

Material Damage

Property damage from a single mud slide can reach hundreds of millions of dollars. Houses in affluent parts of Los Angeles have been buried or carried away by mud slides. But in general, the poorer the area, the poorer the construction, and the greater the damage. In underdeveloped countries, entire shantytowns and villages have been destroyed. And damage is not restricted to structures. In agricultural areas, acres of cropland have been ruined.

Prevention

Governments must prohibit new construction and habitation in known mud slide areas. In populated mud slide areas, barriers can be constructed to stop or redirect the flows. Japan, the world leader in mudflow control, has built steel and concrete dams to retard the frequent mud slides on Mount Usu, on the island of Hokkaido. Some villages in Indonesia have constructed artificial hills for people to retreat onto during lahars.

Survival

• If you live in a mud slide area and heavy rains begin, head for high ground. If you find yourself in the path of a mud slide, shed all excess clothing and baggage and try to outrun it. If you are not fast enough, get behind a tree or in a protected corner of a high, solid structure. If you are overtaken by the muck, keep your head up and try to "swim" through it as best you can, but do not thrash or struggle—struggling will only cause the mud to suck you deeper.

RIVER FLOODING

INJURY/ILLNESS/
TRAUMA

CLIMATE

PRIMARY
ENVIRONMENT

VICTIMS

INCIDENCE

MATERIAL DAMAGE

On July 31, 1976, a system of heavy thunderstorms stalled above the headwaters of the Big Thompson River in Colorado. In just 90 minutes, 10 inches of rain fell, and the river rose from 18 inches to 20 feet, a phenomenal increase in volume. A flash flood in the form of a 20-foot wall of water raged down into the Big Thompson River canyon. Thousands of people, mostly campers, scrambled frantically uphill for safety while stout trees were uprooted and cars were swept away by the roaring waters. "The violence of the water was indeed hard to believe," recalled witness Cynthia Ramsay. "It smashed a 2-story municipal power plant at the foot of the canyon into a pile of brick rubble, and reduced a concrete bridge to gravel."

As violent and harrowing as the Big Thompson River flash flood was, it was but a minor incident compared to some of the truly catastrophic river floods that have occurred throughout history. The worst river flood disaster in modern history took place in August 1931, when China's Hwang Ho River—also known as "China's Sorrow"—burst its banks, killing approximately 3.7 million people. Less than a decade later, in 1939, all of northern China's rivers overflowed at the same time, killing 500,000 people, with millions more perishing in the famine that followed.

The worst river flooding in North America occurs along the lower Mississippi River in the states of Arkansas, Mississippi, Tennessee, and Louisiana. Waters from 50 tributaries (including the Ohio, Missouri, Minnesota, and Arkansas rivers, major waterways in themselves), draining more than 1 million square miles of land, flow into the 2,348-mile-long Mississippi River. During a flood, the Mississippi may rise to 30 times its normal level. The most severe Mississippi River flooding occurred in 1927, when 26,000 square miles of land were inundated. During relief work, rescue boats cruised among the treetops, plucking survivors from branches and roofs.

Name/Description

River floods have a variety of causes, including the structural collapse of a dam or the accidental damming or choking of a river by a landslide or ice, but the primary cause is rain. Sudden, sporadic rain from storms, or seasonal rains, often compounded by water from melting snow and ice in the spring, cause rivers to overflow their banks. Because of the weight of water—one cubic foot of water weighs 62 pounds—and its ability to flow swiftly, the destructive energy of even a moderate flood is immense.

Injury/Illness/Trauma

In the United States, floods now kill more people annually than any other weather-related phenomena. The recent increase in flood fatalities is attributed to continued settlement of flood-prone areas. Most fatalities in floods are caused by drowning. Other victims are battered to death as they are swept along or bludgeoned to death by fast-moving debris. Floodwaters often contaminate freshwater sources, leading to disease among survivors, who may also be subject to malnutrition or starvation if crops and food supplies have been destroyed. (See Injury/Illness/Trauma, page 104.)

Material Damage

Floodwaters, often carrying mud and solid debris, can easily sweep away all but the most solidly anchored objects and structures, including trees, houses, bridges, cars, and trucks. The muddy waters may also ruin crops, food stores, machinery, appliances, yards, streets, and the interiors of houses and buildings. The annual cost of flood damage in the United States exceeds $3 billion.

Prevention

Potential flood areas must be identified and protected, especially in places where developers are planning to build new communities. Along the flood-prone Mississippi River, 1,700 miles of levees (embankments to prevent flooding) with an average height of 27 feet have been built, and there are an additional 2,000 miles of levees along its tributaries (making the levee system longer than the Great Wall of China). Soil and forest conservation can be helpful; forestlands absorb much of the runoff from storms before the excess water can reach nearby rivers.

River Flooding

When China's Hwang River flooded in 1931, 3.7 million people drowned.

Survival

- If you find yourself in a flood-prone area during heavy rains or other flood conditions, get to high ground as quickly as possible.

- If you are caught inside a house or building during a flood, close all doors and windows and stay upstairs or in the attic. Make sure you have access to the roof. (See Disaster Preparation and Survival, page 106.)

SNOW

INJURY/ILLNESS/
TRAUMA

CLIMATE

PRIMARY
ENVIRONMENT

VICTIMS

INCIDENCE

MATERIAL DAMAGE

"Christmas, 6 P.M. It is fearfully cold and raw and a snowstorm is setting in. The wind is northeast and beats in the faces of the men. It will be a terrible night for the soldiers who have no shoes. Some of them have tied old rags around their feet, but I have not heard a man complain." Those words were written by one of General George Washington's aides on Christmas Day, 1776, and they describe one of the many cruel days and nights endured by the ill-equipped Continental army during the winter of 1776–77. (Later that night, despite the nasty weather, Washington and his troops made their famous crossing of the Delaware River and successfully attacked the British garrison at Trenton, New Jersey.)

Snow

Harsh winters and the snows they bring are as much a part of American history as George Washington and the crossing of the Delaware. The United States has the dubious honor of having experienced the world's heaviest recorded snowfalls. The heaviest seasonal snowfall yet recorded—83 feet—occurred at the Paradise Ranger Station in Mount Rainier National Park in Washington State during the winter of 1956–57. The greatest single-day snowfall yet recorded was 74 inches at Silver Lake, Colorado, April 14, 1921.

Name/Description

Snow is defined as precipitation in the form of small, white ice crystals formed directly from the water vapor of the air at a temperature of less than 32 degrees Fahrenheit. One-third of the earth's surface is touched by snow during a single year, and permanent snow and ice cover 12 percent of the globe. In regions such as the Arctic, where snow is omnipresent, it plays a significant role in the culture of the local inhabitants. The Inuit of the far north have many different words for snow; the words refer to the various kinds of snow they recognize. The distinctions are often very subtle and would not be recognized by a non-Inuit. The Inuit word *I-gluk-sak*, for example, refers to a certain kind of snow that is ideal for the building of igloos.

Generally—that is, outside of Inuit society—two basic kinds of snow are recognized. Snowflakes that are formed in the humid atmosphere of coastal or maritime regions are wet, which allows them to bond together when they collide, forming large, heavy, conglomerate snowflakes. The largest snowflake on record was 2.4 inches across (although there were reports of 8 inch by 12 inch snowflakes falling at Bratsk, Siberia, during the winter of 1971). Snowflakes that form inland, away from large bodies of water, are dry, which prevents them from bonding, and thus they are usually smaller than wet snowflakes. Snowflakes fall in a seemingly infinite variety of crystalline shapes, including stars, plates, prisms, and needles.

Dangerous Natural Phenomena

Injury/Illness/Trauma

Many of the fatalities attributed to snow each year are traffic related. There are also a substantial number of deaths caused by heart attacks during and after snowstorms, usually suffered by people shoveling snow, pushing stuck cars, and walking through deep snow. Other fatalities may be attributed to exposure and hypothermia. Bruises, fractures, and broken bones from falls are very common in snowy areas; the elderly are most susceptible to these kinds of injuries. Snow blindness, a temporary but painful sensitivity to light, can be caused by prolonged exposure to the intense glare of the sun on the snow. (See Injury/Illness/Trauma, page 104.)

Material Damage

Snow is tremendously expensive to remove and dispose of. It can cause costly delays for travelers and transporters of goods. Snow, especially wet snow in large quantities, is quite heavy and does considerable damage to highways, bridges, and other structures. Roofs of houses and buildings often cave in under the weight of snow. In 1982 in Cardiff, Wales, the roof of the city's largest entertainment center collapsed after a heavy snowfall.

Prevention

Heavy, wet snowstorms are the hardest to predict because they occur under conditions in which a slight change in temperature can turn a snowstorm into a rainstorm, and vice versa. The National Weather Service gives fairly accurate snow predictions and winter storm warnings. In areas where deep snowdrifts tend to accumulate, snow fences have proved effective. Natural snowdrift barriers, such as hedges or rows of trees, can also be used for this purpose.

Snow

**The greatest single-day snowfall yet recorded was 74 inches
at Silver Lake, Colorado, on April 14, 1921.**

Survival

- During a snowstorm, stay indoors. If you must go outside, wear layers of clothing and avoid heavy exertion. (See Disaster Preparation and Survival, page 106.)

SUBSIDENCE

INJURY/ILLNESS/
TRAUMA

CLIMATE

PRIMARY
ENVIRONMENT

VICTIMS

INCIDENCE

MATERIAL DAMAGE

"It was the strangest sound I ever heard," recalled Mae Rose Owens of Winter Park, Florida. "It was like a giant beaver eating away the earth." Walking out the front door of the house she had lived in for 35 years, Owens saw that a large hole had suddenly appeared in her yard. It grew steadily bigger, swallowing up full-grown oak trees. Mae Rose Owens began packing. She moved out the next day, just hours before the house joined the oak trees. The sinkhole continued to grow, severing underground water pipes and power lines, nibbling at a nearby laundry and a print shop, and devouring five cars and a camper. Eventually, it grew to be 400 feet wide and 125 feet deep.

Subsidence

On November 21, 1970, villagers in Runjh, northern India, were awakened by a deep rumble and the vibration of their huts. Rushing outside, they found a gaping hole where a bamboo grove had been. The hole was about 60 feet in diameter. An even larger sinkhole appeared one night in Kansas, swallowing a small-town railroad station. In Dublin, Virginia, a 25-foot sinkhole engulfed several coffins in a cemetery. They had to be dug out and reburied. And in Lakeland, Georgia, a parking lot suddenly vanished, leaving behind a crater 80 feet in diameter and 30 feet deep.

Name/Description

Subsidence is the sinking or collapsing of the ground in a certain area. The result of severe ground subsidence is a sinkhole. Subsidence can occur quickly and dramatically, with no warning, or it can occur gradually, over a period of many years. A good example of gradual subsidence is the Leaning Tower of Pisa, in Italy. Since its construction began in 1173, gradual subsidence has caused the famous tower to lean precariously. Subsidence can occur on a limited scale, as was the case with Mrs. Owen's house in Florida, or it can occur on a massive scale; the entire city of Venice, Italy, is currently subsiding.

The most common form of ground subsidence develops in areas where underground water flows through weak rock such as limestone, and even weaker gypsum and salt rock, carving out subterranean caverns with arched roofs. These arches, and the earth above them, are supported by the underground water. If the underground water level drops, the cavern roofs become weak and collapse, resulting in subsidence and sinkholes. Subsidence can also occur in mining areas, where networks of abandoned mines fill with water and eventually weaken and collapse. During the 19th century, primitive salt mining techniques used in Cheshire County in England resulted in ongoing, extensive subsidence. Houses, roads, fields, and canals subsided. By the 1880s,

A sinkhole in Winter Park, Florida, grew to 400 feet wide and 125 feet deep and devoured five cars and a camper, among other things.

about 50 years after the salt mines had been abandoned, the town of Dunkirk was threatened. "Houses overhang the street as much as two feet, whilst others lean on their neighbors and push them over," one witness wrote. "The area of mischief is extending yearly."

Injury/Illness/Trauma
Fortunately, the earth's rumbling and the creaking noises of moving structures give ample warning to people in the vicinity of a relatively sudden subsidence event. Injuries are for the most part insubstantial.

Subsidence

Material Damage

Material damage caused by subsidence is extensive and costly. Subsidence can damage or destroy houses, buildings, streets, highways, parking lots, bridges, vehicles, and agricultural land, among other things.

Prevention

If potential trouble spots can be detected beforehand, civil engineers can usually prevent subsidence from occurring, usually by raising underground water levels. The problem is detection. Limestone caves, for example, are hard to find without expensive drilling. Infrared photography and microwave radiometry can detect variations in ground temperature and water distribution that relate to cave patterns, but these techniques are expensive.

Survival

- If you find yourself near a subsidence event, whether you are in your house or elsewhere, vacate the area immediately.

THUNDERSTORM

INJURY/ILLNESS/
TRAUMA

CLIMATE

PRIMARY
ENVIRONMENT

VICTIMS

INCIDENCE

MATERIAL DAMAGE

Just about everyone has experienced a violent, frightening thunder-storm—the polar regions are the only places on earth where they do not occur—but the most harrowing stories come from aviators, who frequently have close encounters with these airborne maelstroms.

During a gliding competition in the Rhön Mountains in central Germany in 1938, five contestants deliberately flew their gliders into a storm cloud in search of thermals (rising masses of warm air). They found what they were looking for. Sucked violently upward through the thunderheads, the flimsy aircraft disintegrated. The pilots bailed out and pulled the rip cords on their parachutes. But the updrafts seized the parachutes and the helpless men were rocketed upward through freezing winds, rain, hail, and lightning. "It is difficult to imagine the ordeal of the others," stated the only survivor. "At a height of over 10 kilometers (6.2 miles), they must have been frozen, tossed about like living icicles."

In August 1959, Lieutenant Colonel William Rankin of the U.S. Marine Corps bailed out of his jet fighter when its engine failed at 46,000 feet above the South Carolina coast. Rankin plummeted 10,000 feet directly into "the boiling pot of a thunderstorm" before his parachute deployed. Once the parachute opened, he was at the mercy of the violent air currents, which jerked him up and down at a mile per minute through the churning storm, while lightning flashed around him and he was pelted with hail and rain. "I was jarred from head to toe," Rankin wrote of his 45–minute ordeal. "Every bone in my body was rattled. . . . as though some monstrous cat had caught me by the neck and shaken me."

Name/Description

The word *thunder* comes from the Old English *thunor*, which is akin to the name of the Norse god of thunder, Thor. Thunder is the sound that follows a flash of lightning (see Lightning, page 60); it is caused by the sudden expansion of the air in the path of the electrical discharge. A thunderstorm is a local, short–lived storm system characterized by towering cumulonimbus clouds, or thunderheads, high winds, heavy precipitation, and often severe thunder and lightning. Thunderstorms harbor enormous amounts of energy, which is expended in the form of lightning, thunder, wind, rain, and hail. Summer presents the most favorable conditions for thunderstorms. Heating of the earth's land surface promotes thermals, or rising currents of warm, moist air. In summer, when the thermals contain a lot of moisture, they form cumulus clouds, which are further lifted when they encounter a cold front or, on occasion, a mountain range. Massive, towering cumulonimbus clouds are then formed; developing within these clouds are storm cells containing violent updrafts and downdrafts of moisture–laden air. These storm cells unleash the heavy precipitation, high winds, and spectacular thunder and lightning associated with thunderstorms. A large thunderstorm with a number of storm cells may be several miles wide and long and may roil up to an altitude of 50,000 feet. Occuring most often during late afternoons or evenings in the summer, thunderstorms can spawn tornadoes (see Tornado, page 88) and cause flash floods (see River Flooding, page 72).

Injury/Illness/Trauma
The variety and degree of injuries caused by thunderstorms is enormous. Victims can be drowned in floods, struck by lightning, burned in fires caused by lightning, injured by hail, or battered by windblown debris. (See Injury/Illness/Trauma, page 104.)

Material Damage
Thunderstorms cause extensive material damage. The bulk of this damage is related to flooding and mud slides caused by heavy rains, and fires caused by lightning. In the United States alone, an estimated 10,000 forest and brush fires are started by lightning annually. High winds, and especially thunderstorm–related winds known as microbursts—violent downdrafts that spread out laterally upon hitting the ground and achieve velocities of over 100 miles per hour—are also responsible for a significant amount of damage. (Microbursts are particularly dangerous for aircraft during takeoffs or landings.)

Prevention
The National Weather Service relies on a variety of sources for thunderstorm prediction, including radar, satellites, balloons, aircraft, and

Thunderstorm

**One thunderstorm has the energy equivalent
of 13 Nagasaki-type atomic bombs.**

sophisticated computers for analysis of meteorological conditions and
patterns. The service's Severe Local Storm Forecast Center at Kansas City,
Missouri, monitors weather conditions 24 hours a day.

Survival

• See Hail, page 45; Hurricane, page 49; Lightning, page 60; Mud Slide,
page 68; River Flooding, page 72; Tornado, page 88; and Disaster
Preparation and Survival, page 106.

TORNADO

INJURY/ILLNESS/
TRAUMA

CLIMATE

PRIMARY
ENVIRONMENT

VICTIMS

INCIDENCE

MATERIAL DAMAGE

By all accounts, there is nothing like the fury of a tornado. The attempts of witnesses—perhaps *survivors* is a more appropriate word for these people—to describe this phenomenon testify to the terrible power and destructive energy involved.

Before the appearance of a tornado (or a swarm of tornadoes), an eerie, humid stillness falls over the countryside. As a towering wall of thunderheads approaches, the sky is often said to turn a strange, greenish color. The storm breaks, howling winds and sheets of rain and hail lash the streets and fields, and there are dazzling displays of lightning and deafening thunderclaps. The tornadoes appear—whirling funnels that look like "gigantic elephants' trunks" or "wide, solid columns" reaching down from the mass of dark clouds to touch the earth. The

Tornado

sound made by an approaching tornado is compared to "the roar of ten thousand freight trains" or the "thunder of a million cannons." What happens during those brief moments when a tornado actually touches down in a populated area is, in fact, indescribable. Those who live through the event can only describe the aftermath: "In a twinkling of an eye . . . all was gone."

The single most destructive tornado in history was the so-called Tri-State Tornado of March 18, 1925. The tornado first appeared in the early afternoon in southeast Missouri. It headed northeast, growing larger and larger and leaving wrecked towns in its wake. By the time it crossed the border into Illinois, the black funnel was a mile wide, and its roar could be heard for miles. Witnesses said that the tornado seemed to be filled with lightning. It continued its destructive march across Illinois and then passed into Indiana, where it annihilated the town of Griffin before finally dying out near the town of Princeton, which also sustained heavy damage. The tornado's rampage had lasted for three hours; four towns were completely destroyed, and 689 people were dead. The bodies of some victims—broken, naked, and caked with black grime—had been carried for miles before the tornado released them.

Name/Description

Tornado is derived from the Spanish word for thunderstorm, *tronada*. A tornado is a vortex of extremely violent winds whirling about a concentrated area of extremely low atmospheric pressure. Tornadoes are formed in thunderstorm cells when violent updrafts of warm, moist air acquire a tight, cyclonic momentum, producing winds of up to 350 miles per hour—the strongest winds known.

Although tornadoes occur in Europe, Asia, Africa, Australia, and South America, they are most common in North America, and especially in the infamous Tornado Alley, a broad region of the Great Plains that includes parts of Texas, Oklahoma, Missouri, Kansas, and Nebraska. Central Oklahoma is the most tornado-prone area in the world. Tornado

Alley is most active in the late spring and early summer, when masses of warm, moist air from the Gulf of Mexico encounter cool, dry air blowing across the continent from the north and west, resulting in powerful thunderstorms. These thunderstorms spawn tornadoes, which can appear singly or in swarms.

The first visible indication of an approaching tornado is a funnel cloud extending downward from the cumulonimbus clouds of a severe thunderstorm. A tornado can become quite dark from the debris sucked into its vortex. Although their motions can be wildly erratic, tornadoes usually travel on a northeasterly course at about 35 miles per hour. They often "leap" or "skip" across the countryside, touching down in one place, lifting up for a few miles, and then touching down again. Thus they usually leave discrete pockets or narrow bands of devastation in their wake. Not all the destruction is caused by the tornado's winds: the low-pressure field that surrounds a tornado acts like a vacuum, sucking the air from buildings and houses. If there are not enough open doors and windows in a house or building for the air inside to escape through, the structure can literally explode.

Injury/Illness/Trauma

A tornado can inflict injuries of every imaginable kind. (See Injury/Illness/Trauma, page 104.)

Material Damage

Tornadoes can cause billions of dollars worth of damage in a single year.

Prevention

Meteorologists cannot pinpoint where a tornado will touch down. They can only predict the likelihood of the formation of tornadoes, follow their movements on radar once they appear, and issue warnings and alerts based on this information.

Tornado

**The sound of an approaching tornado has been compared to
"the roar of ten thousand freight trains."**

Survival

- If a tornado is approaching, open some windows and then be sure to stay away from them.

- If you are in a house with no storm cellar, go to the basement and huddle in the corner nearest the approaching tornado. If there is no basement, stay on the ground floor under a piece of heavy furniture near the center of the room.

- If you are caught out in the open, try to get away from the tornado by moving away from the tornado's path at right angles. If you are overtaken, lie in a ditch, ravine, or similar depression and protect your head.

TSUNAMI

INJURY/ILLNESS/
TRAUMA

CLIMATE

PRIMARY
ENVIRONMENT

VICTIMS

INCIDENCE

MATERIAL DAMAGE

The legend of the lost continent of Atlantis concerns an ancient but highly civilized culture that vanished when the alleged continent mysteriously sank to the bottom of the Atlantic Ocean. It is now believed that the legend of Atlantis was at least partially based on actual events that occurred in the Aegean Sea around 1375 B.C. According to records kept by ancient Egyptian scholars, a volcanic island named Thíra, located about 140 miles southeast of Athens, erupted suddenly, causing a gigantic seismic wave, or tsunami, to slam into the Minoan island of Crete. The wave, estimated to have been 165 feet high, "wreaked such havoc that the Minoan civilization was destroyed."

A more modern tsunami occurred in August 1883. It was set off by a volcanic explosion that obliterated the South Pacific island of Krakatau (see Volcano, page 96). With a force comparable to that of a thermo-nuclear explosion, the eruption set off a tsunami that raced across the Indian Ocean at speeds of up to 400 miles per hour. Walls of water 120 feet high rolled into Sumatra and neighboring islands, destroying 163 villages and killing 40,000 people. Ships were carried inland for miles by the great waves.

Name/Description

Tsunami is a Japanese word; *tsu* means "overflowing" and *nami* means "wave." Tsunamis are often called seismic sea waves or tidal waves, although they have nothing to do with tides. A tsunami is a series of ocean waves of great length and long duration. They are usually generated by underwater earthquakes or volcanic activity.

On the open sea, tsunamis are long and low; they may be only a few feet high, which makes them almost impossible to detect from onboard a ship or from the air. As tsunamis approach shallow waters around coastlines, friction with the sea bottom reduces their velocity. But the friction also shortens the length of the waves and makes them pile up to great heights. Thus, by the time a tsunami hits land, it may be well over 100 feet high.

Occasionally, the imminent arrival of a tsunami is heralded by an odd phenomenon—a kind of artificial low tide that occurs when the approaching sea wave sucks coastline waters toward it, sometimes exposing the sea bottom near the shore. During such an occurrence in Portugal on November 1, 1755, crowds of curious but unwary people

In August 1883, a tsunami moved across the Indian Ocean at speeds up to 400 miles per hour, creating 120-foot waves.

wandered out onto the newly exposed seabed. Minutes later, they were all gone, obliterated by a wall of water.

Injury/Illness/Trauma
See River Flooding, page 72.

Tsunami

Material Damage

The destructive power of a tsunami is comparable to that of an earth-quake. These apocalyptic waves can obliterate everything in their path, with the most severe damage occurring along the coastline.

Prevention

After a disastrous tsunami hit Hawaii in 1946, the Pacific Tsunami Warning System was established among the Pacific nations.

Survival

• If a tsunami warning is issued, get as far inland as possible as quickly as you can.

VOLCANO

INJURY/ILLNESS/
TRAUMA

CLIMATE

PRIMARY
ENVIRONMENT

VICTIMS

INCIDENCE

MATERIAL DAMAGE

In 1783, the volcano Laki, located 120 miles east of Iceland's capital, Reykjavík, erupted. Ten thousand people, along with three-quarters of Iceland's domestic livestock, perished. Lava (molten rock) covered 200 square miles of land, and volcanic ash damaged crops 500 miles away in Scotland. Ash and smoke from the eruption clouded skies in the Northern Hemisphere for months, causing Benjamin Franklin to write about "a constant fog all over Europe and a great part of North America."

When the volcanic island of Krakatua erupted on August 27, 1883, it hurled five cubic miles of debris into the air. Ash obscured the sun, turning day to night, and fell from the skies like a black snow over a 300,000-square-mile area. Ash suspended in the stratosphere created **spectacular** sunsets for several years, inspiring the English poet Alfred

Volcano

Lord Tennyson to pen, "For day by day thro' many a blood red eve . . . The wrathful sunset glared."

There was many a blood red eve in the Pacific Northwest after the 1980 eruption of Mount St. Helens in Washington State. The volcanic mountain, part of the Cascade Range of the Rocky Mountains, had last erupted in 1857. This time, the eruption was so violent that one side of the 10,000–foot mountain was blown off, triggering a landslide of unprecedented proportions. Five miles away, a geologist monitoring the volcano had time to shout "This is it!" into his microphone before he was swept away, never to be seen again. The eruption of Mount St. Helens annihilated virtually every living thing within a 230–square–mile radius.

Name/Description

The word *volcano* is derived from the Latin *Vulcanus*, the Roman god of fire. A volcano is a vent in the earth's crust through which rocks, ash, hot gases and vapors, and lava are released. Volcanoes occur on the ocean floor as well as on land. A volcano often develops into a mountainous cone formed from the hardened material ejected from the vent.

Volcanic eruptions are caused by the buildup of tectonic heat and pressure (see Earthquake, page 29). If a volcano has been dormant for an extended period, a cap of hardened rock forms over the vent. Superheated rock, hot gases, and steam driven upward from cracks in the earth's crust are blocked from escaping by a capped vent, and enormous amounts of pressure and energy accumulate. Minor earthquakes and deep rumbling sounds can be felt and heard in the vicinity of the volcano during this period, and sometimes the cone can be seen to bulge outward as the pressure grows. When the pressure becomes too great, the volcano blows its cap off in a massive, fiery explosion that spews lava, gas, rocks, and ash for miles in all directions. A major volcanic eruption represents one of the most powerful expenditures of energy to occur on this planet.

Injury/Illness/Trauma

Volcanic eruptions are responsible for a variety of particularly gruesome ways to die. Some victims are killed by falling debris or burned to death in fires caused by flowing lava. Others are poisoned by gases belched from the volcano during the eruption; still others are killed by the intense heat, which can cause clothes to burst into flame spontaneously and can shrink human bodies "as if most moisture had been extracted from them." Death usually comes quickly and suddenly. After the eruption of Martinique's Mount Pelée, the body of a clerk was discovered, "bending over a ledger, pen still in hand, frozen in the immobility of death." Another corpse was "bent over a washbasin from which the water had evaporated." And "some who had evidently staggered a few steps, lay with contorted bodies, hands clutching at scalded mouths and throats."

Material Damage

The power of a volcanic eruption is devastating. The initial shock wave from the Mount St. Helens blast felled 130,000 acres of trees. Super-hot lava flows destroy everything in their path. Burning debris raining from the sky can start intense fires miles away from the volcano. Gigantic floods, avalanches, landslides, and mud slides obliterate entire towns at a volcano's base. Tsunamis set in motion by an eruption threaten coastline and island communities. Billowing clouds of volcanic smoke and ash drift great distances and remain suspended in the stratosphere for years, disrupting ecosystems and weather patterns and endangering food resources.

Prevention

Geologists and volcanologists have developed sophisticated devices and techniques for detecting and predicting imminent eruptions. Even the relatively sudden and unsuspected eruption of a dormant volcano can

Volcano

**The 1980 eruption of Mount St. Helens blew off one side
of the 10,000-foot mountain, triggering a landslide.**

usually be detected in time for evacuations of threatened areas. Lava flows that threaten houses and towns can often be deflected, halted, or channeled into uninhabited areas by civil engineers.

Survival

- If there is time, get as far away as possible.
- If you are in a place that is receiving heavy smoke and ash, your body should be fully covered, and goggles and a surgical mask should be worn.

WIND

INJURY/ILLNESS/
TRAUMA

CLIMATE

PRIMARY
ENVIRONMENT

VICTIMS

INCIDENCE

MATERIAL DAMAGE

In English, it is known as wind, but there are at least 400 other names for this omnipresent phenomenon. And *wind* is a rather general term; there are many words that characterize very specific kinds of winds. There is the mild chinook wind of the eastern Rocky Mountains, welcomed in winter because of its warmth. Residents of Southern California, on the other hand, dread the arrival of the hot, dry Santa Ana winds, which originate in the Mojave Desert and are notorious for fanning

Wind

brush fires into major infernos. A similar wind known as the Brickfielder occurs in Australia. The cold mistral wind blows down from the Alps to chill the Mediterranean coast. The sirocco is a burning wind that blows north out of the Sahara Desert. The sirocco is as hot and debilitating as a high fever; under the Turkish Ottoman Empire, murder was often pardonable if it was committed during the sirocco.

Occasionally, freak winds materialize, causing havoc and an almost superstitious fear. In 1095, an "outrageous wind" destroyed 600 houses in London and carried off the roof of Bow Church. On November 7, 1940, an "uncanny wind" blowing across Puget Sound, Washington, caused the newly built Tacoma Narrows Bridge to undulate wildly and eventually collapse. And in 1925, the "wind of the century" blew out of the Irish Sea, rushed across Europe at 125 miles per hour and blew all the way to Iran, leaving 20 dead and hundreds injured. The highest wind speed ever recorded occurred atop Mount Washington, New Hampshire, on April 12, 1934, when an anemometer registered a 231-mile-per-hour gust.

Name/Description

Winds are masses of air in motion. Because of the earth's spherical shape, the equator receives most of the heat from the sun. Winds occur as the atmosphere attempts to redistribute this warm air to all parts of the globe. These planetary wind systems, which generally move from the equator toward the poles, are further affected by the rotation of the earth, by passage over geographical features such as mountains, deserts, and oceans, and by interaction with cooler masses of air, giving birth to regional or localized winds and the accompanying weather systems and storms. (See Blizzard, page 14, Cyclone, page 18, Hurricane, page 49, Monsoon, page 64, Thunderstorm, page 84, and Tornado, page 88).

Wind velocities are measured according to the Beaufort scale. Invented by Admiral Francis Beaufort in 1805, the scale originally referred

Structural damage begins to occur when winds reach forces of 47 to 54 miles per hour, force 9 on the Beaufort scale of wind velocity.

to the amount of sail a vessel could safely use in specific wind conditions. The Beaufort scale runs from force zero (winds less than 1 mile per hour) to force 12 (winds of more than 72 miles per hour).

Injury/Illness/Trauma

Winds can cause injuries varying in severity from minor (see Dust Devil, page 26) to fatal (see Tornado, page 88).

Wind

Material Damage

According to the Beaufort scale, structural damage begins to occur when winds reach force 9—47 to 54 miles per hour. At force 10—55 to 63 miles per hour—considerable structural damage occurs. At force 11—64 to 72 miles per hour—there is widespread damage, and at force 12—73 miles per hour and above—damage can be catastrophic.

Prevention

Today, using sophisticated computer projection techniques and an increasing number of weather satellites and radar installations, meteorologists have achieved a better than 90 percent accuracy for 24-hour predictions of most wind systems and the weather they bring. However, prediction time is significantly reduced as wind and weather systems become volatile.

Survival

- See Blizzard, page 14; Cyclone, page 18; Dust Devil, page 26; Hurricane, page 49; Thunderstorm, page 84; and Tornado, page 88.

APPENDIX I:
Injury/Illness/Trauma

Every year, millions of people around the world are adversely affected by dangerous natural phenomena. Primary physical injuries caused by these events range from mild to severe to fatal. Secondary physical effects are usually related to the widespread disease and malnutrition that often follow a major natural disaster. Perhaps the most long lasting damage resulting from such disasters is psychological. Physical wounds and ailments usually heal much more quickly than emotional ones.

Injury

The majority of injuries attributed to natural disasters are commonly seen throughout the entire spectrum of catastrophic occurrences. Broken bones, fractures, abrasions, sprains, contusions, and lacerations of varying severity are the most common injuries, and they can be inflicted during the course of almost any kind of dangerous natural phenomenon. Injuries can be caused directly, usually by falling or flying objects, and they can be caused indirectly—frantic or panicked people often injure themselves during catastrophic events. If the injuries are serious, they may be accompanied by shock, a condition characterized by the failure of the circulatory system to maintain an adequate blood supply to vital organs. Heart attacks are also a common occurrence during any stressful event. Certain less generalized kinds of injuries are specifically related to distinct phenomena. Drownings, of course, occur during flash floods and storm surges. Electrocution and accompanying burns are a threat during thunder–and–lightning storms. Burns are also frequently associated with volcanoes, as are respiratory damage and asphyxiation from hot, poisonous vapors and gases. Hypothermia (low body temperature) is most often associated with blizzards and snow avalanches.

Illness

A major natural disaster can injure and kill people outright; it can also destroy, cut off, or contaminate food and water supplies, causing widespread and long-lasting malnutrition and starvation, as well as diseases such as typhoid and dysentery. Disease and starvation are often responsible for as much if not more suffering and death than the primary effects of the event. This is especially true in underdeveloped parts of the world, where food, medicine, and necessary medical and rescue equipment are in short supply in the first place, and where relief efforts are often poorly planned and coordinated.

Trauma

Victims of natural disasters often suffer from the symptoms of psychological trauma long after the disaster itself has passed. Disaster victims often experience profound feelings of helplessness and loss of control over their own environment, and these feelings can leave deep emotional scars. Disasters that occur suddenly, with little or no warning—such as earthquakes, tornadoes, and avalanches—inflict the most severe psychological wounds. Survivors of such disasters often find that their emotional foundations of security and well-being have been acutely undermined.

The array of long-lasting and often debilitating symptoms that plague many survivors of natural disasters are usually grouped under the heading of disaster syndrome or post-traumatic stress disorder (PTSD). The initial symptoms of PTSD are emotional numbness and detachment. More severe symptoms may not appear until months after the disaster. These symptoms include irritability, hostility and anger, depression, social withdrawal, anxiety, paranoia, insomnia, nightmares, disorientation, headaches, shortness of breath, trembling, heart palpitations, sweating, dizziness, and exhaustion. Some victims experience flashbacks to the traumatic event.

Following the Vietnam War, thousands of young Americans returned home from Southeast Asia only to be tormented by PTSD caused by the violent horrors of that conflict. In order to help Vietnam veterans, psychologists and physicians began developing methods to relieve the symptoms of PTSD and to eliminate the disorder itself. Today, these methods are successfully utilized to treat people who suffer from PTSD related to all kinds of traumatic events and experiences, from child abuse to earthquakes. Treatments include support groups, various medications, behavioral modification techniques, and psychotherapy.

APPENDIX II:
Disaster Preparation and Survival

Preparation

- Stock up on nonperishable foods such as canned and freeze-dried goods. Lay in a supply of drinking water and/or water purification tablets.

- Keep a complete first-aid kit handy. Make sure bandages, disinfectants, and analgesics are included. If someone in your family requires regular medication, such as insulin, make sure there is an adequate supply.

- Prepare for a loss of power. Extra clothing, blankets, candles and/or oil lamps (always be careful with candles, especially indoors, and have a fire extinguisher on hand if possible), matches (sealed in plastic bags to keep out water), flashlights, fuel for a fireplace or a camp stove, a battery-operated radio, and an emergency toilet may be required. Make sure you have plenty of fresh batteries. Extra gasoline for vehicles may be needed.

Survival

- Keep your radio or television tuned to a station that maintains emergency broadcasts. Follow instructions; if authorities advise evacuation, take their advice. A large percentage of natural disaster–related injuries and fatalities can be attributed to people refusing to leave their homes despite direct instructions to do so.

- If you are sick or elderly, avoid exertion.

- Avoid going outside, especially after dark. If you must go out, it is best not to travel alone. Always take a flashlight at night. Be sure to avoid downed power lines.

Appendix II

- Beware of using an open flame if there is a possibility that gas lines are damaged.
- Never eat anything that has been in contact with flood water; it may be contaminated.
- Avoid damaged buildings.
- If you must enter a flooded basement where electrical appliances are located, be sure the power is off.
- Report any broken water, sewer, or gas pipes and lines, as well as fires and downed power lines.
- Help your neighbors.

FURTHER READING

The American Medical Association's Handbook of First Aid and Emergency Care. New York: Random House, 1980.

Arnold, Peter. *Check List for Emergencies.* New York: Doubleday, 1974.

Cable, Mary. *The Blizzard of '88.* New York: Atheneum, 1988.

Goodman, Jeffrey. *We Are the Earthquake Generation: Where and When Catastrophes Will Strike.* New York: Seaview Books, 1978.

Halacy, Daniel Stephen. *Ice or Fire? Surviving Climatic Change.* New York: Harper & Row, 1978.

Knapp, Brian. *World Disasters/Drought.* Austin, TX: Steck Vaughn Library, 1990.

———. *World Disasters/Storm.* Austin, TX: Steck Vaughn Library, 1990.

Ludlum, David M. *The Weather Factor.* Boston: Houghton Mifflin, 1984.

Raphael, Beverly. *When Disaster Strikes.* New York: Basic Books, 1986.

Stommel, Henry M. *Volcano Weather: The Story of 1816, the Year Without a Summer.* Newport, RI: Seven Seas Press, 1983.

INDEX

109

Dangerous Natural Phenomena

Index

Missy Allen is a writer and photographer whose work has appeared in *Time, Geo, Vogue, Paris-Match, Elle,* and many European publications. Allen holds a master's degree in education from Boston University. Before her marriage to Michel Peissel, she worked for the Harvard School of Public Health and was director of admissions at Harvard's Graduate School of Arts and Sciences.

Michel Peissel is an anthropologist, explorer, inventor, and author. He has studied at the Harvard School of Business, Oxford University, and the Sorbonne. Called "the last true adventurer of the 20th century," Peissel discovered 14 Mayan sites in the eastern Yucatán at the age of 21 and was the youngest member ever elected to the New York Explorers Club. He is also one of the world's foremost experts on the Himalayas, where he has led 14 major expeditions. Peissel has written 14 books, which have been published in 83 editions in 15 countries.

When not found in their fisherman's house in Cadaqués, Spain, with their two young children, Peissel and Allen can be found trekking across the Himalayas or traveling in Central America.

ACKNOWLEDGEMENTS
The authors would like to thank Linda Siri for her meticulous research, and Sally Lee for her phenomenal help.

A VISIT TO
WILLIAM BLAKE'S INN

POEMS FOR INNOCENT
AND EXPERIENCED
TRAVELERS

A VISIT TO

POEMS FOR INNOCENT

WILLIAM BLAKE'S INN

AND EXPERIENCED TRAVELERS

BY NANCY WILLARD

ILLUSTRATED BY
ALICE AND MARTIN PROVENSEN

METHUEN CHILDREN'S BOOKS
LONDON

FOR RALPH, WHO BUILT THE INN,
AND FOR ERIC, WHO LOVES BLAKE

First published in Great Britain in 1982 by Methuen Children's Books Ltd.,
11 New Fetter Lane, London EC4P 4EE.

Reprinted before publication

Text copyright © 1981, 1980 by Nancy Willard
Illustrations copyright © 1981 by Alice Provensen and Martin Provensen

ISBN 0 416 22160 2

PRINTED IN THE UNITED STATES OF AMERICA

"Will you come?" said the Sun.
"Soon," said the Moon.
"How far?" said the Star.
"I'm there," said the Air.

PLEASE RETURN

WM.
BLAKE'S
INN

CONTENTS

INTRODUCTION TO
WILLIAM BLAKE'S INN

I was seven and starting my second week in bed with the measles when I made the acquaintance of William Blake.

"Tell me a story about lions and tigers," I said to the baby-sitter. Although it was nearly nine o'clock, I had no desire to sleep.

Miss Pratt, the sitter, looked up at the ceiling on which my father had glued stars that glowed in the dark. Then she said, very softly, a poem that began:

> *Tyger, Tyger, burning bright*
> *In the forests of the night,*
> *What immortal hand or eye*
> *Could frame thy fearful symmetry?*

"Did you make that up?" I asked, astonished.

"No," said Miss Pratt. "William Blake made it up."

"Does he live close by?"

"He died nearly two hundred years ago," said Miss Pratt. "Lights off. I'm going downstairs."

Two days later there arrived in the mail a little book with wonderful pictures: *Songs of Innocence* and *Songs of Experience* by William Blake. I am almost sure Miss Pratt sent it. I say almost, because on the title page, in flourishing script, was the following inscription:

> *Poetry is the best medicine.*
> *Best wishes for a speedy recovery.*
>   *yrs,*
>   *William Blake*

NANCY WILLARD

WILLIAM BLAKE'S INN
FOR INNOCENT AND EXPERIENCED TRAVELERS

This inn belongs to William Blake
and many are the beasts he's tamed
and many are the stars he's named
and many those who stop and take
their joyful rest with William Blake.

Two mighty dragons brew and bake
and many are the loaves they've burned
and many are the spits they've turned
and many those who stop and break
their joyful bread with William Blake.

Two patient angels wash and shake
his featherbeds, and far away
snow falls like feathers. That's the day
good children run outside and make
snowmen to honor William Blake.

WILLIAM BLAKE ENGRAVER POET & PAINTER

BLAKE'S WONDERFUL CAR
DELIVERS US WONDERFULLY WELL

The driver bowed and took my things.
He wore a mackintosh and wings.

He wore a mackintosh and boots
the tender green of onion shoots,

and on his cap, in dappled green,
was "Blake's Celestial Limousine."

My suitcases began to purr.
"Your luggage is excessive, sir.

All luggage must be carried flat
and worn discreetly on your hat

or served with mustard on a bun."
Alarmed, I said I hadn't one.

My suitcases, my fondest hopes
grew small and pale as envelopes.

"Now all aboard and all at ease.
I only carry whom I please."

Uneasily I stepped inside
and found the seats so green and wide,

the grass so soft, the view so far
it scarcely could be called a car,

rather a wish that only flew
when I climbed in and found it true.

A RABBIT REVEALS MY ROOM

When the rabbit showed me my room,
I looked all around for the bed.
I saw nothing there
but a shaggy old bear
who offered to pillow my head.

"I was hoping for blankets," I whispered.
"At home I've an afghan and sheet."
You will find my fur soft
as the hay in your loft,
and my paws make an admirable seat.

"I was hoping to waken at sunrise.
 At home I've an excellent clock,
 a lamp, and a glass
 through which the hours pass,
 and what shall I do for a lock?"

I will keep you from perilous starlight
and the old moon's lunatic cat.
When I blow on your eyes,
you will see the sun rise
with the man in the marmalade hat.

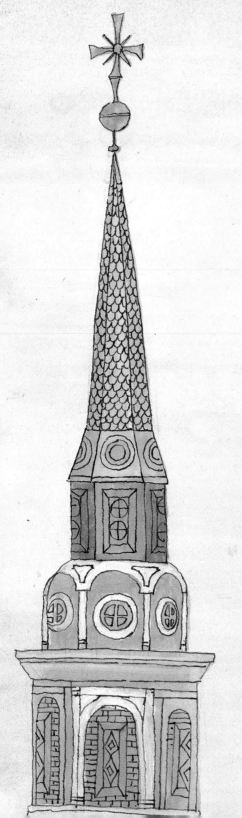

THE SUN AND MOON CIRCUS
SOOTHES THE WAKEFUL GUESTS

That night the tiger rose and said,
"What is this rumbling overhead
    that robs me of repose?"

To which the rabbit made reply,
"The moon is entering the sky,
    a-twirling on her toes."

The King of Cats sprang up in fright.
"What is this fitful flashing light
    that will not let me sleep?"

The rabbit said, with perfect tact,
"The sun is opening his act
    and crouching for a leap."

I rang the bell above my bed
so loud I thought I'd wake the dead.
    "Rabbit," I called, "come here!"

"No need," he said, "to cry and quake.
Two ancient friends of William Blake
    have come to bring us cheer."

Three sunflowers, in earthen beds,
stood up and slowly turned their heads
    with patience unsurpassed.

The old sun danced, the new moon sang,
I clapped my hands; the morning rang
as creatures clapped with paw and fang,
    and fell asleep at last.

The man in the marmalade hat
arrived in the middle of March,
equipped with a bottle of starch
to straighten the bends in the road, he said.
He carried a bucket and mop.
A most incommodious load, he said,
and he asked for a room at the top.

Now beat the gong and the drum!
Call out the keepers
and waken the sleepers.
The man in the marmalade hat has come!

The man in the marmalade hat
bustled through all the rooms,
and calling for dusters and brooms
he trundled the guests from their beds,
badgers and hedgehogs and moles.
Winter is over, my loves, he said.
Come away from your hollows and holes.

Now beat the gong and the drum!
Call out the keepers
And waken the sleepers.
The man in the marmalade hat has come!

THE KING OF CATS
ORDERS AN EARLY BREAKFAST

Roast me a wren to start with.
Then, Brisket of Basilisk Treat.
My breakfast is "on the house"?
What a curious place to eat!
There's no accounting for customs.
My tastes are simple and few,
a fat mole smothered in starlight
and a heavenly nine-mouse stew.

I shall roll away from the table
looking twice my usual size.
"Behold the moon!" you will whisper.
"How marvelous his disguise.
How like the King of Cats he looks,
how similar his paws
and his prodigious appetite—
why, in the middle of the night
he ate, with evident delight,
a dozen lobster claws."

"Where did you sleep last night, Wise Cow?
Where did you lay your head?"

"I caught my horns on a rolling cloud
and made myself a bed,

and in the morning ate it raw
on freshly buttered bread."

TWO SUNFLOWERS

MOVE INTO THE YELLOW ROOM

"Ah, William, we're weary of weather,"
said the sunflowers, shining with dew.
"Our traveling habits have tired us.
Can you give us a room with a view?"

They arranged themselves at the window
and counted the steps of the sun,
and they both took root in the carpet
where the topaz tortoises run.

THE WISE COW
MAKES *Way*, *Room*, AND *Believe*

The Rabbit cried, "Make *Way!*
Make *Way* for William Blake!
Let our good poet pass."
The Wise Cow said, "Alas!
Alack! How shall I make
a thing I've never seen?
To one that lives on grass
what's good is green.
Therefore I must make *Way*
of grass and hay,
a nest where he can nap
like fieldmice in a cap."

The Rabbit cried, "Make *Room!*
Make *Room* for the marmalade man!
He is mopping and mapping the floors.
He is tidying cupboards and drawers."
The Wise Cow said, "Can I
make *Room* and *Way* together?
To one that lives outdoors
what's good is weather.
Therefore I must make *Room*
like a bright loom.
The marmalade man can weave
good weather, I believe."

The Rabbit cried, "Make *Believe*,
and make it strong and clear
that I may enter in
with all my kith and kin."
The Wise Cow said, "My dear,
Believe shall be a boat
having both feet and fins.
We'll leave this quiet moat.
We'll welcome great and small
with *Ways* and *Rooms* for all,
and for our captain let us take
the noble poet, William Blake."

He gave silver shoes to the rabbit
and golden gloves to the cat
and emerald boots to the tiger and me
and boots of iron to the rat.

He inquired, "Is everyone ready?
The night is uncommonly cold.
We'll start on our journey as children,
but I fear we will finish it old."

He hurried us to the horizon
where morning and evening meet.
The slippery stars went skipping
under our hapless feet.

"I'm terribly cold," said the rabbit.
"My paws are becoming quite blue,
and what will become of my right thumb
while you admire the view?"

"The stars," said the cat, "are abundant
and falling on every side.
Let them carry us back to our comforts.
Let us take the stars for a ride."

"I shall garland my room," said the tiger,
"with a few of these emerald lights."
"I shall give up sleeping forever," I said.
"I shall never part day from night."

The rat was sullen. He grumbled
he ought to have stayed in his bed.
"What's gathered by fools in heaven
will never endure," he said.

Blake gave silver stars to the rabbit
and golden stars to the cat
and emerald stars to the tiger and me
but a handful of dirt to the rat.

WHEN WE COME HOME, BLAKE CALLS FOR FIRE

Fire, you handsome creature, shine.
Let the hearth where I confine
your hissing tongues that rise and fall
be the home that warms us all.

When the wind assaults my doors
every corner's cold but yours.
When the snow puts earth to sleep
let your bright behavior keep

all these little pilgrims warm.
They who never did you harm
raise their paws a little higher
and toast their toes, in praise of fire.

Tiger, Sunflowers, King of Cats,
Cow and Rabbit, mend your ways.
I the needle, you the thread—
follow me through mist and maze.

Fox and hound, go paw in paw.
Cat and rat, be best of friends.
Lamb and tiger, walk together.
Dancing starts where fighting ends.

THE KING OF CATS
SENDS A POSTCARD TO HIS WIFE

Keep your whiskers crisp and clean.
Do not let the mice grow lean.
Do not let yourself grow fat
like a common kitchen cat.

Have you set the kittens free?
Do they sometimes ask for me?
Is our catnip growing tall?
Did you patch the garden wall?

Clouds are gentle walls that hide
gardens on the other side.
Tell the tabby cats I take
all my meals with William Blake,

lunch at noon and tea at four,
served in splendor on the shore
at the tinkling of a bell.
Tell them I am sleeping well.

Tell them I have come so far,
brought by Blake's celestial car,
buffeted by wind and rain,
I may not get home again.

Take this message to my friends.
Say the King of Catnip sends
to the cat who winds his clocks
a thousand sunsets in a box,

to the cat who brings the ice
the shadows of a dozen mice
(serve them with assorted dips
and eat them like potato chips),

and to the cat who guards his door
a net for catching stars, and more
(if with patience he abide):
catnip from the other side.

William, William, writing late
by the chill and sooty grate,
what immortal story can
make your tiger roar again?

When I was sent to fetch your meat
I confess that I did eat
half the roast and all the bread.
He will never know, I said.

When I was sent to fetch your drink,
I confess that I did think
you would never miss the three
lumps of sugar by your tea.

Soon I saw my health decline
and I knew the fault was mine.
Only William Blake can tell
tales to make a tiger well.

Now I lay me down to sleep
with bear and rabbit, bird and sheep.
If I should dream before I wake,
may I dream of William Blake.

BLAKE TELLS THE TIGER
THE TALE OF THE TAILOR

There was a tailor built a house
of wool of bat and fur of mouse,
of moleskin suede, the better part
of things that glimmer, skim and dart.

Of wood and stone the man professed
his ignorance. He said, "It's best
to work with what I know.
Shears, snip. Thread, go.
I'll have a house in the morning."

The tailor and his wife moved in
and lined it well with onionskin.
Of velveteen they made the chairs,
and snails' feet and comets' hairs.

Of bricks and boards the man professed
his ignorance. He said, "It's best
to work with what I know.
Shears, snip. Thread, go.
I'll have a house in the morning."

And when that pair lay down to sleep,
cries and chirps conspired to keep
the tailor and his wife awake.
"Husband, since we cannot take

fur and fury, wool and wings
back to those who lost these things,
back to those from whom we stole
wool of bat and skin of mole,
let us leave this house and take
rooms at the inn of William Blake."

Of ghostly griefs, the man professed
his ignorance. He said, "It's best
to work with what I know.
Shears, snip. Thread, go.
We'll go to Blake's in the morning."

That night the winds of April blew
the tailor's house apart, askew,
and the wet wind who once went bare
wore wool of bat and comet's hair.

He made their bed of robins' wings
caught, with other flying things,
in a low trap of twigs and lime.
It was the tailor's own design.

Of nails and knotholes he professed
his ignorance. He said, "It's best
to work with what I know.
Shears, snip. Thread, go.
I'll have a house in the morning."

On windy days and moonless nights,
Blake wears a suit of shifting lights.
The tailor now has grown so clever
he stitches light and dark together.

"Now sun and sparrows, take your rest.
And farewell, friendly trees. It's best
to work with what I know.
Shears, snip. Thread, go.
All things are new in the morning."

My adventures now are ended.
I and all whom I befriended
from this holy hill must go
home to lives we left below.

Farewell cow and farewell cat,
rabbit, tiger, sullen rat.
To our children we shall say
how we walked the Milky Way.

You whose journeys now begin,
if you reach a lovely inn,
if a rabbit makes your bed,
if two dragons bake your bread,
rest a little for my sake,
and give my love to William Blake.

BLAKE'S ADVICE TO TRAVELERS

He whose face gives no light
will never become a star.

William Blake

—from "Proverbs of Hell,"
The Marriage of Heaven and Hell
by William Blake